Center of Gravity / Gev

M000222482

Cei

One woman's experiment to reinvent her entire life
through creativity, spirituality and a leap of faith.

Geva Salerno

Center of Gravity / Geva Salerno

Levity Press
21301 S. Tamiami Trail #320-130
Estero, FL 33928

Printed in the United States of America

The Library of Congress registered Center of Gravity on
April 24, 2013
Registration Number TXu 1-864-899

ISBN-13: 978-0991099412
ISBN-10: 0991099419

Cover Design: Geva Salerno and Susanna Wohlpart

www.gevasalerno.com

Prologue

The last time I spoke with Bryan, neither one of us wanted to get off the phone. We had been together for almost two years and we knew it would be the last time we spoke...probably forever. I was leaning over the desk on my back porch overlooking the lake, elbows propped up on the desk and my feet wrapped around the base of the chair.

We both knew it was the end. I had warned him that we needed to break up several times over the past few months. He had just acknowledged it and didn't say much. I presume that he felt there wasn't much he could do to change the situation. He knew I wanted children and a family and he very clearly did not. I wished he would fight me on it, but he didn't.

We had come to this stalemate and broken up once about a year prior, but I could only stay away from him for two days before going back. Maybe he thought I wasn't serious, that I'd eventually go back to him again... like the last time. No... not this time.

Over the past year, we had enjoyed our time together but there was always that looming issue standing between us. It felt like the relationship wasn't going anywhere. And wanting, but not starting a family was eating away at the back of my mind until I couldn't stand it anymore.

Maybe he thought I was bluffing again, but during the last week I cut down on the times we saw each other or spoke, until there we were on the phone having our last conversation as a couple. "I love you, B." "I love you too, G." "Bye." "Bye." And then it was over. The cord was cut and the balloon floated away.

It was three days before Valentine's Day. Who breaks up with someone three days before Valentine's Day? ...I felt like a rat. But, I really believed in love. I couldn't stand the thought of going through Valentine's Day with the "I love yous" and the cards and the flowers and the pretending everything was fine. I could not even remotely picture it.

I cried for hours off and on after we got off the phone. But, I wasn't sad on Valentine's Day. I love love and I felt like I had stood up for real love by ending it. And so the day felt somewhat buoyant.

But as the law of physics tells us, what goes up must come down. And for the next year and a half, I was obsessed with thoughts of dating and men and the future, falling deeper and deeper into a state of confusion about my life, my relationships, and my sense of self. But, On October 1st 2011, something changed. I began a year-long experiment which ultimately changed my life.

Introduction

It was late September and I was driving along Golden Gate Parkway on my way to work. I was thinking about my ex-boyfriend Bryan, wondering what he was up to - debating for the thousandth time whether to contact him or not - when an interview with a scientist came on the radio. He was discussing new research on brain usage.

Apparently, the old myth about using only 10% of the brain was misleading. According to the research, we use all of our brain, just not all at the same time. It occurred to me how much time I spent thinking about Bryan and men in general, versus time spent thinking about my own life and my own interests - literally thousands of hours - wasted. The parkway was busy and I had to swerve to avoid hitting a sedan that had slowed. The research was intriguing. If we only use 10% of our brain at any one time, I was probably using my little 10% thinking about men almost continuously.

Regardless of the persistent sun, my mood became gloomier and gloomier the closer I got to the office. I felt trapped and constricted by the thought of sitting in front of a computer for eight hours. I was wasting my brainpower at work and I was wasting it outside of it as well. If I wasn't thinking about the future and what kind of mate I wanted, I was on the computer perusing singles ads and responding to emails.

I felt like time was getting shorter and shorter. It was all about finding a man before it was too late. I wasn't even sure what "too late" was exactly, but I was sure it was sometime within the next few years. I was in my early forties and the quiet ticking of my biological clock was a constant companion. I didn't even want to bear children really. I was actually more interested in adoption. But the thought that I would soon have no choice in the matter bothered me. And I didn't really want to adopt a child by myself either.

I came to a stop light and stared in the rearview mirror. I wondered if I would suddenly become unattractive in a few years. Supposedly, women of a certain age (what age was that exactly?) were no longer in demand. I thought I looked pretty good. Would I wake up one day and look in the mirror and see some older, tired, useless version of myself staring back? And what about those ridges between my eyes? They had formed over the last few years in response to the multitude of small and large stresses. I kind of looked angry even when I wasn't.

I looked away from the mirror and back at the traffic in front of me. I felt like a door was slowly sliding shut. I wanted to run up and stick my shoe in the crack to prevent it from closing all the way. It seemed like finding a mate was the only answer. I had to find someone to hook up with and make a life with before it was too late.

And so there was the stream of mismatched, blind dates that were the result of my very thorough internet dating searches. In order to support the process, I had come up with a rather detailed description of the type of man I was looking for and an equally detailed description of myself. Then I edited it down to the following:

Him: Kind, Smart, Family-Oriented, Funny, Enjoys Sports, Dynamic, Hard-Working, Wide Variety of Interests, Take Charge Type...

Me: Smart, Successful, Adventurous, Likes to Travel, Dressing up or Quiet Nights at Home, Prefers a Man to Arrange the Date...

Regardless of the specificity, the men who responded to the ads were extremely varied. Every day I would arrive home and immediately log on to see who had responded. I was always encouraged by the number of replies and always held out hope that one of them was "the one." But it had become just one disappointment after another. After breaking up with Bryan, I had gone on 18 blind dates and not one of them was a match. Yes, they were all nice in their own way and they all had at least one quality that attracted me. But, none of them resembled the man in my description.

I wasn't being petty or superficial. I accepted a date with a 300-pound man who had a great sense of humor. But when I was talking about how I loved to roller blade, he asked if I was afraid of falling. Okay, I *never* fall when rollerblading. His question was a complete turn-off, both because I resented him putting a thought like that in my head and because I wanted a man who was at least as brave as me.

Then there was the good-looking fireman. I showed up wearing a pretty, blue dress and he showed up wearing a huge chip on his shoulder. And, I couldn't quite understand his sense of humor. Was he mocking me? And what was up with the story he told about one of his dates getting naked on his couch when he stepped out of the room for a moment? It was all too bizarre. What started as an interesting search became an endless parade of strange characters.

I turned left and headed onto Goodlette Road. Most of the time at work, I didn't think about dating too much. But, even there the thoughts would creep in. I would be in the middle of preparing a proposal and suddenly I would think about my ex-boyfriend or a potential date or I'd start wondering what I was doing that weekend. I definitely didn't want to be alone on a Saturday night.

So there I was driving along, when it hit me. I needed to take my life back! *This is ridiculous*, I thought. *I need to get rid of all of these thoughts of men and marriage and children. Maybe then things will change. Maybe then I'll be able to recapture my life.*

When I arrived at work, I switched into work mode. But when I got home that night, I started to conceptualize an experiment. I would stop focusing on men and clear my head. But, it would have to be long enough to make a lasting impact. My birthday was only a few days away. Maybe if I gave up dating for one whole year...

What would it be like to take a year off from all of that relentless focus on dating? What would it be like to just concentrate on my own life? It made sense to me to design it as an experiment, considering that one of my intellectual adventures had consisted of getting a biochemistry degree. Since graduating, the degree had been pretty useless due to the fact that I found the actual practice of science to be completely boring.

Part of me was definitely fascinated by science. Over the years, I had read at least a half dozen biographies

4

of scientists. I was fascinated by how they could focus on something for so long and spend so much time alone. And my first boyfriend, Stevie was a scientist. Or maybe he was just a kid who collected bugs...

Stevie was seven and I was six. He collected all kinds of dead bugs, which he kept in a plastic box with little labels on each bug. My dad called him the "Bug Man." One time when we were walking in the woods I made him sit on a hill next to me. I leaned over and said "Kiss me."

"What?" He said looking shocked.

"You know like on TV," I said. I closed my eyes and waited. Suddenly, it felt like someone pressed a wet frog up against my lips. I must have had a horrified look on my face, because he got up and ran away.

Other than Stevie and his bugs, I really had no exposure to science growing up. My family was into art and music and making leather goods. We had parties with my parents' colorful group of friends at our farm house out in the country. My parents weren't into things like numbers and math and how things work.

When I got to high school, the first class that actually stumped me was chemistry. I had been sailing along at the bottom of the "top class," when suddenly I was getting left behind. Everybody seemed to understand chemistry, but me. I couldn't get it. I even had to stay after school for help. I had never felt stupid before.

Regardless of excelling in almost every subject, I never really fit in with that "top class." And chemistry I really had to work at. At that point, I had started identifying myself as an artist anyway, wearing eclectic clothes and wild makeup, dressing the way I thought an artist would

5

dress. Art class was actually fun. We got to try all different mediums, like raku and jewelry making.

Toward the end of my junior year, some of the cool kids were talking about college. I leaned over the back of my chair and asked Tonya Ippolito what she planned to study. "Probably chemistry or biology," she said. I was in awe. I didn't even know what to say to that. She went back to chatting with her friends.

When my family and I moved in my senior year, I had no real plan for the future. My art teacher encouraged me to apply to art school. I felt proud of the pieces I was creating, so I went ahead and applied to a prestigious art school she suggested. I was accepted, but had no idea how to pay for it. I shelved that idea and went to work, getting a real estate license, waiting tables and cutting hair.

Six years later, when I decided I really wanted a college degree, I didn't know what to study. Everything was equally interesting to me. I could have just as easily majored in anthropology, psychology, or economics. But I wanted something I would be proud of, something worthwhile... something like science.

I wasn't sure that a career in science wasn't for me. But I knew I needed a bachelor's degree to do anything interesting with my life and I wanted to prove it to myself and the world that I could get a degree in science. Probably the ultimate would have been to a get degree in physics, but I wasn't that courageous. I started studying chemistry, which again surprised me with its level of difficulty. When things got tough, I just kept going.

After two semesters, I saw an advertisement for the biochemistry program and switched, thinking it might be easier. The program was definitely interesting. I was on the edge of my seat in some of the classes, like physical chemistry and cell biology. I would ask a million questions in classes where everyone else seemed bored to death. But to me the actual labs were boring. And scary. I was never prepared properly and I never knew what was going on.

It was while I was interning at the EPA as an undergrad that I did a little water quality work at a lab, which cemented my decision to never work in a lab. I kind of liked collecting water samples from a boat, but my supervisor had me count colonies of e-coli in petri dishes which was completely boring. I kept losing track and coming up with different numbers. I wanted to tear my hair out.

I worked very, very hard as a student, literally spending 9 to 11 hours straight, studying... sometimes for days on end. I would get to the point where I thought I understood the material well enough to take the test, only to receive a D or an F. I had to repeat Physics One and I ended up taking Physics Two three times. But I never gave up. I never even contemplated giving up. When faced with a failure my question was always "what do I do now?" Somehow, there was always some way to keep going. And then suddenly, I was done.

But this kind of an experiment was interesting to me. Maybe if I just removed this one variable - *men* - something major would happen. I figured a year would be long enough to entirely change my life and to internalize whatever habits were necessary to maintain a more healthy focus afterward.

It had to be cold turkey. No dating, no sex and no men for one year... a vow... a vow of celibacy? Well, yes. But, the experiment would be so much more than a vow of celibacy. The no sex thing would not be a problem because I hadn't had sex in just about a year anyway. I knew that because the last man I was with was Bryan on my birthday, a pathetic attempt to connect with someone long after breaking up.

If I had not dated much or had much sex in the last year, how would the next year be any different? Where was the experiment in that? The major difference was that although I hadn't dated much in the last year, I had thought about it a lot, brooded... worried... and basically obsessed over dating... *very* attractive. This year - no thinking about men!

Admittedly part of me wanted to do the experiment for just that reason – to become more attractive. I had recently read The 28 Laws of Attraction by Thomas Leonard and it certainly influenced me. I had been in a bookstore six months prior casually looking for another book when this one caught my eye. I turned away, but something brought me back to it a couple times until I finally felt compelled to pick it up.

The subtitle of The 28 Laws of Attraction is "Stop Chasing Success and Let it Chase You." The book espoused the theory that if you work on your life and fulfill yourself, success will chase you – money, relationships, whatever you need, will come to you. I had read it avidly, a little at a time over the course of six months and had already put many of the principles into action.

However, something wasn't working. Maybe I needed more time to focus on my life? That meant spending less time obsessing over men.

Supposedly, the scientific method has been practiced for over one thousand years by all kinds of scientists. It requires that a study question be formed, followed by a hypothesis, then a prediction and rigorous testing. I would love to say that I followed it. But, in reality the process was far more intuitive. If I had a study question, it was "how can I possibly change my life?"

My path was not a straight ahead, logical path. I had only a murky understanding of what was to be done. Often, I felt like a detective trying to solve a mystery by following clues. Sometimes, the clues were easy to spot because they were left for me in wise books like the 28 laws of Attraction. Other times, I had no clues and it was more like searching for bread crumbs, which I had left behind for myself long ago. And sometimes, I was just following my intuition.

In many ways, I was like a very tired swimmer, desperately afraid of drowning, trying to keep my head above water and following only a faint outline of the shore ahead. If I had thought it out clearly and articulately, my hypothesis would have been: "If I fill up my life with activities and friends, I will no longer think about men."

I suppose a second hypothesis was "If I no longer think about men, I will become more attractive." And my prediction was "if I become attractive to men, I will automatically meet the right man," leading to the final prediction that "upon completing the experiment, I would meet Mr. Right and I would live happily ever after."

But, again the actual thought process was closer to "I need to give up thinking about men for a year." And so I did. No one could have guessed that the results of the experiment would be so radically different than the prediction.

Center of Gravity / Geva Salerno

Chapter One
The Birthday Party

October

On October 1st I woke up late, rolled over and grabbed the new journal with the bright blue butterfly on the cover. It had been lying there next to the bed for the better part of a year, waiting for me to find a reason to write in it. Over the last few years, I had been taking notes whenever something particularly compelling or noteworthy happened. I realized that my life had become so boring that I had literally nothing to write about.

Well, today was different. I opened the hard-covered journal and started describing the experiment. There weren't a lot of rules, except for this one: no dating. I didn't really know how the experiment would go. I would have to make it up as I went along. One thing was sure, I would actively try to change my life.

Currently, my life is boring and draining: work, work, work and one long obsessive search for a man, I wrote. I flipped the page and described how even though I had read Thomas Leonard's 28 Laws of Attraction, and had actively tried to improve my life, there were still huge holes. I had unconsciously tried to fill them holes with things like shopping, but to no avail.

My intention was to fill the holes with experiences and activities that I enjoyed. Perhaps there were clues in my past. I would explore some of the activities I had enjoyed in my youth but had put away as I grew up. I would just put one foot in front of the other and see what happened.

Putting the journal aside, I decided to get ready for my birthday party at the beach. My entire walk-in closet was filled with work clothes: many, many dark suits, dresses and blouses. The little closet across from it contained my casual clothes, an odd array of items I had picked up at different times.

As usual, I rifled through the choices not finding anything suitable. There were sundresses that were pretty, but too revealing, some I had never worn. There were pin-striped clam diggers, which looked like fun but never seemed quite right.

And there were also about 20 tee shirts. I felt like I should wear tee shirts. Everybody wears t-shirts. But in reality I never wear tee shirts. No matter what the shape, they never fit my body type - short and voluptuous. There were two different beach cover ups, both of which were too sexy for a family event. I grabbed my bathing suit and threw on a tank top and shorts.

As I drove to the beach, I wondered if I should tell my family about the experiment or not. *Probably not.* I was in the habit of keeping my dreams close until they manifested. I didn't want to share the experiment with anyone yet. And what if I changed my mind? What if after a few weeks or months, I was overcome with the desire to date again?

Maybe I would get so lonely I wouldn't be able to stand it. *Not likely.* I was sure this was the right time. I was so sick and tired endlessly thinking about men. My mind was a mouse on a wheel and it was time to jump off.

At Parking Area 4 of the Wiggins Pass Beach, I noticed my parents' car parked in the last space at the end, under a canopy of sea grape trees. They were unloading beach toys, umbrellas, table cloths, and grocery bags. Everything was spilling out onto the boardwalk.

My mom's floppy hat flew off in the breeze, letting loose her wild, grey curls. My dad ran to retrieve the hat, his flip flops clacking on the pavement as he chased after it. I parked the car and helped them bring the items to the shady picnic area bordering the beach. A Hispanic family was set up at the picnic table across the way, and my sister Grae was at our picnic table setting out platters of vegetables and chips with her two year old in tow. She was simultaneously trying to set things out and keep Weston occupied. Her long, curly hair was tied back severely. She was only two years younger than me. She had become so serious over the years. *What happened to that wild child I used to know?* I wondered.

Various family members buzzed around, setting up for the celebration. This was my vision. But there was something slightly off about it. Everyone had suggested different options, including a girls' night out and a house party. What I really wanted was a family day at the beach...something low key. I wasn't even sure whom I would invite to a girls night out, other than my three sisters. This was the first birthday since I stopped hanging out with my three girlfriends: Sylvia, Kaitlin and Katy.

The last time the four of us had all hung out was in Puerto Rico, six months prior. None of them had met each other before the trip. They were each my friends, and I thought it would be cool to get them all together and take a girls vacation.

Individually, I liked them all, but for different reasons. They were all smart. Sylvia was kind of artsy and off-beat. She reminded me of Boston, our mutual hometown. Kaitlin was very smart, independent and sophisticated, always jetting off to New York City. I knew Katy from my nonprofit work. She was from Chicago and somehow always brought out my sense of humor. Whenever we were together we would laugh and laugh about the crazy nonprofit world. I felt a stab of longing, thinking of my old friends.

We had gotten together to discuss travelling over dinner. They all seemed to get along, so we started planning a trip to Puerto Rico. The trip went fabulously. I was so burned out and exhausted that I really didn't want to do any of the more adventurous activities with Sylvia and Kaitlin, like hiking the rainforest or Kayaking in the bioluminescent bay.

I just wanted to lie on the beach and casually check out the shops. Katy had a bad hip and various health problems so we took the easy track. But, each night we all met up for dinner and had a great time. My friends got to know each other and back home even started to hang out together.

After the trip, I started to wonder what these three women had in common. They each seemed to represent a part of me: Boston, humor, art... But was there something else? Sylvia, who was so outgoing, had put aside a career as a photographer to make jewelry. She was shut up in a room, alone, all day. Kaitlin worked in a support role for her father's company, unable to express her true talents as a

14

leader and professional because her father didn't see her as worthy. And Katy, I had coached for years to quit a job in an abusive environment, which finally ended with her being let go anyway.

I realized that each of them were afraid of manifesting and expressing their true selves in different ways. They all seemed like weak women. Was that what we had in common? Was I weak, too? The thought had terrified me.

I had thought about how the people around you influence who you become and decided I would have to let them go. But it seemed to be mutual. As I was letting them go, they seemed to be letting go of me as well. Now here I was, six months later, not knowing who I would even invite to my own birthday party. *Maybe this experiment is a bad idea, I thought.*

At the picnic area, everyone seemed to be doing their own thing. I couldn't figure out what I was supposed to do. My youngest sister Garan arrived with her husband and Liam, my two-year old nephew. *They're all so blond*, I thought with a chuckle. Garan was the only blond in our Italian-looking family.

Liam skipped off to the beach immediately. I decided to follow. As I made my way through the path and onto the boardwalk, the hot sand stung the bottom of my feet. The sun was half-way down in the sky and the afternoon light illuminated the nearly empty beach.

My dad had set up beach chairs at the crest of the sand overlooking the water. Terry, brother-in-law, was entertaining my curly-haired niece in one of the chairs. He jumped around in front of her and she laughed at his terrible jokes the way only a four year old would. I smiled and sat down.

At the edge of the sea, my nephew Dalton was racing back and forth, trying to outwit the tide. I couldn't remember ever being that young and innocent. Down the beach I noticed a nice-looking Hispanic man and two women out in the water. They were floating on inflatable rings and laughing. Just out of ear shot, it seemed that the heavier woman was flirting unrepentantly.

My attention kept coming back to the man down the beach. *Why does my mind drift back over there?* I thought. It felt like an addiction, like being addicted to a substance you had to have. There wasn't even anything special about the guy… I sat down in one of the chairs and thought about what it might be like to take a whole year off from dating. *Would I really be able to break this addiction?*

My eyes drifted back to the man in the water. He reminded me of Carlos, whom I had divorced five years earlier. Prior to meeting Carlos, I had been ambivalent about getting married, never really able to picture it. But one evening when I was in Mexico doing volunteer work, I looked out over the glowing city from the four story balcony of my room and thought *What an incredible adventure I'm having... but I have no one to share it with. Is that how my life is going to be? A series of amazing adventures that I have, alone?*

For some reason, as I looked out over the city, I started to imagine that I was standing at a podium, about to make a speech. There was a man by my side, holding one of our two children. That's what I wanted: a strong partner by my side. Maybe being married wouldn't be such a bad idea after all…

I met Carlos about three weeks later. I was standing outside the Teatro de La Republica in Queretaro, Mexico, where the original Mexican Constitution was signed. The theatre was two stories high and occupied the entire corner of the intersection. Around me a swarm of Catholic school children was waiting to get inside. It was my day off from volunteering at El Puente de Esperanza, and I was burned out on my volunteer work. I wanted to visit some historical sites to better understand Mexico, and to start to enjoy myself.

I thought I'd wait a few minutes and let the children go through. As I turned to look back at the street, a man passed by and said "Buenos dias." "Buenos dias," I replied. "Como estas?... How are you?" he said and we chatted for a few minutes. He looked to be in his late twenties or early thirties. His complexion was neither Spanish nor Indian. One of his eyes was brown, the other dark blue.

He asked if he could join me for a tour and we went inside. I was so taken off guard that I barely noticed the guitar he was carrying. We took the stairs up to the second floor and went through a little door that opened onto the balcony overlooking a grand theatre below, which was completely empty. Below to our left, the stage was set with empty orchestra chairs. We sat down and he pointed out that the grand chandelier hanging from the ceiling was a gift from Maximillian de Hapsburg's mother. She had sent it from France when her son was emperor of Mexico for a few years.

We chatted about our homes, his in Puerta Vallerta, mine in the states. Then he asked if I'd like to hear a song. He proceeded to play the guitar and sing a song that sounded romantic to my untrained ears. I could make out about half the words, but I couldn't really concentrate on them because I was still taken aback by being alone in a beautiful theatre with a mysterious stranger.

Afterward, we walked along the cobblestone streets and he shared some of Queretaro's history. That began a whirlwind romance and one of the best weeks of my life, with Carlos bringing me to museums, parks, and parties every day. One night around 10 pm he led me to a park where men wearing big round hats and black suits with silver buckles were standing around holding guitars. Carlos paid them to play for us and asked me to dance. As he whirled me around the park, I thought "Now, this is the kind of man I could spend my life with."

What the hell was I thinking? Life is not a party. Who chooses a husband based on fun? I turned my attention back to the beach and decided to go back to the picnic area. Garan, my youngest sister was hanging decorations from the palm trees and the sounds of surf and sea gulls enfolded us. I nibbled on the deviled eggs my mom had prepared for me, one of the few party foods my restrictive gluten-fee, vegetarian diet allowed.

I took a deep breath and let it out slowly. My family was milling about. In the not so distant past, our family events were fraught with tension and outbursts that seemed to come out of nowhere. It had always reminded me of the proverb about the two rooms: In one room people were seated at a table in front of a big bowl of soup, but were crying out in agony from hunger. They had spoons but the spoons were too long for them to reach their mouths. In the next room, the scene was similar with a group around a big bowl of soup. But, in this room, the people were happily feeding each other.

Not in my family. In my family, there was an underlying need to fight for resources and attention. Many a family holiday ended with an argument breaking out and someone storming off. Often, it was Giselle. Sometimes, it was Garan, my youngest sister and occasionally it was one of my parents. Many times, Giselle took something the wrong way and then the situation would escalate until there was screaming, slamming of doors and car wheels squealing.

The last holiday that was ruined was my birthday party four years prior, when Giselle had walked in the door and been there less than five minutes when she had gotten into a fight with Garan. The noise level quickly went up several decibels and before anyone even realized what was happening, Giselle had turned around and walked out, slamming the door behind her. I stood there, not knowing what to say.

God, I hated family events. I used to dread the holidays. But over the past few years things had improved. Giselle seemed happier in her self and in her life. Everyone seemed a bit more settled and family events were becoming calmer. Garan, came over and sat down next to me at the picnic table. "Happy Birthday, sister," she said. "Thanks. I think it's going to be a good year."

Chapter Two
Fashion

The following week I tried to figure out my next steps. *What should I do first?* I wanted to fill my time and get back to what inspired me. The moment I saw the advertisement for the "Art Walks the Runway" fashion show, it spoke to me of long-forgotten dreams. When I was about 12 years old, I had an English teacher who would always bring in fashion magazines to read on her break. At that time we lived in a small farm town and the magazines seemed to be from another world. I noticed them on her desk and asked if I could see one. Not only did she graciously allow me to read one, but she started saving the issues for me to take home after she finished them.

Sprawled out on my bedroom floor, I would devour the dazzling publications. I loved how the still new, glossy pages felt as I turned from one glamorous scene to the next. They transported me from a simple farm town to a place where beauty and aesthetics mattered. I could see how lines and color were used to evoke a feeling. I could see how a dash of creativity made an outfit, but too much became overwhelming.

Very quickly, I developed not only an eye for style, but also a sense for how fashion could express emotion or whimsy. Of course, I was never able to put any of it into practice. My family was on an extremely limited budget,

20

which did not include fashion. So I absorbed all the beauty and fashion and filed it away mentally. Even so, the magazines continued to be my escape from the drudgery and pain of high school.

The week before the fashion show, I called a few friends to see if anyone wanted to go with me, but, everyone said "no." I was not in the habit of going to large events alone so I kept trying. Everyone I talked to was either too busy being a mom or simply not interested. I didn't know what to do.

As the day approached, my anxiety started creeping in at the thought that I might have to go alone. *Maybe I should hold off and wait for another event,* I thought. In the end, I decided to go by myself and make the best of it. *I have to start doing things that I'm interested in, even if I have to go alone,* I thought

The next hurdle was deciding what to wear. *Does one dress up to fit in with all of the beautiful couture, or dress down so as to not seem to be competing?* Finally, I chose a black dress with wide cut-open sleeves and white and purple flowers along the bottom. I added my favorite long strand of pearls that reached my waist. My hand was shaking a little as I combed my hair back and got ready to leave. I took a deep breath and let it out slowly. *You can do this*, I said to myself, as I spritzed on perfume.

As I walked up the long, marble stairway to the Sydney and Berne Davis Art Center, I wondered what it would be like. *Will I be shunned as an outsider? Will everyone stare at me, knowing that I DO NOT BELONG THERE?*

I handed my ticket to the woman at the door. Inside the large, open space a long, black runway was set up perpendicular to the stage. There were four rows of seats roped off on either side of the stage with "VIP" signs hanging from the velvet ropes. I thought it would be packed, but a lot of the VIP seats were empty. Admission was free and VIP seats were only $10. One of the laws in *The 28 Laws of Attraction* is to over-respond to opportunities and to purchase items with more features than you think you need, so I had bought a VIP ticket. I found my way through the people standing around and located a seat along the stage, feeling very lucky and a little important.

I had always wanted to go to a fashion show and here I was sitting next to the runway! On TV, all the cool people sat next to the runway, taking pictures or fanning themselves with their programs. It was like a dream come true, even if it was only a show in Fort Myers, FL, hardly the fashion mecca of the United States. But it was a real fashion show. The woman next to me was busy chatting with her two friends. *I would like to be chatting with some friends as well,* I thought. But I was content marveling over the fact that I was actually sitting at a real fashion show. Photographers began to gather on a little podium across from the runway and the seats started to fill.

A girl with long, brown hair and a tight silver dress that bloomed out at the hips came out onto the stage and introduced the show. Names of local designers were projected onto the back of the stage as models wearing the various collections came out. I loved seeing the pretty, flowing gowns and I took many pictures. At the intermission, I made my way to the bar on the other side of the room and ordered a glass of sparkling water. *I really don't want to go back and sit by myself,* I thought. *Maybe I'll walk around and look at the art on the walls.*

It seemed that one of the designers was also an artist, as her name was on many of the paintings. Or perhaps the artist was also a designer? There were paintings of mermaid-type women with dayglo stripes down their lengthy gowns. The lights flickered, signaling the end of the intermission and I took my seat. Looking around and fanning myself with the show's program, I smiled at one of the two women taking their seats to my right. She smiled back and continued talking with her companion.

The lights dimmed and the second half of the show began with a model strutting out in a long, black gown that had ruffled circles embroidered down the sides. Another model came out with a big frilly hat and a gown that looked like it had been hand-dyed. The models who followed were all wearing dresses that looked like they had been painted by hand, which is when it dawned on me why the show was called "Art Walks the Runway"—*the gowns are literally works of art, painted by an artist!*

As the last collection was brought out, the lights dimmed to near black, and suddenly there was a model with shocking orange and yellow stripes running through the lower half of a black gown. The colors glowed in the black light. Another model wearing a white gown with hot pink stripes and splash marks came out and replaced the first model. I tried to get the right settings on my camera to keep up with the beautiful colors and styles flowing past me. And then, after many blurred shots and a few good ones, the lights came on. The designer came out and we all clapped. *That was so much fun*, I thought as I made my way to the door and stepped out into the humid evening.

Well, it seemed that the first step in my experiment had a positive outcome. I had successfully attended an event by myself. I had done something that was important to me, regardless of the fact that no one else wanted to go,

23

and I had reconnected with my long lost love of fashion. I was not shunned. I did not die or spontaneously burst into flames. In fact, I was just fine.

***

As difficult as the experiment seemed, I didn't ever want to have another "Carlos" situation again. What had started off well ended up being one long-dragged out annoying chapter in my life.

In the beginning every day was Christmas and every night was the Fourth of July. He was the most attentive, romantic, funny man I had ever dated. We always had fun and we became good friends in Mexico. The only subject we disagreed on was children. He wanted children, as did I, but, I wanted to adopt. This didn't seem like a big obstacle to me. We both basically wanted a family and I figured it would all work out eventually. So, when he proposed marriage, I accepted. Little did I know that his idea of marriage and mine would be so radically different.

After spending five months in Mexico waiting for his visa, travelling by bus through the desert, flying from Texas to Florida, driving from Florida to Massachusetts and working nonstop for two months, he cheated on me. Not technically. It really depends on your definition. But in my family, flirting with a girl and making plans to go to the movies with her counts as cheating.

I was devastated. No one had ever cheated on me before and I had no frame of reference. Two months prior we had married in a civil ceremony at my mother's house. As I had stood putting my makeup on in the bathroom mirror, I thought *This is the time people usually decide whether to go through with it or not. Do I really want to*

24

get married? But, I knew that I had made my decision long before and would abide by it.

Later, when I heard that he had cheated on me, I couldn't believe it. My housemate told me that Carlos had been bothering some girl down at the store. Her father was furious and came by with two pit bulls, threatening to take Carlos apart. Carlos denied it, so I went and spoke to the girl. There, behind the cash register was a fifteen year old girl.

"Could I talk to you for a minute?" I had asked. She looked around nervously.

"Um, okay," she said and followed me outside.

"Listen, this is not your fault. Carlos is a married man and he should have known better. Could you just tell me what happened?"

She assured me that Carlos had come by several times, flirting more and more each time, finally inviting her out to the movies on Friday. Back at home, Carlos confessed. I was forced to decide what to do.

Of course, I couldn't talk with my parents about it. That would be admitting I had made a mistake. I liked having Carlos because he was like a human shield between my family and me. When he was around, I didn't have to deal with any of the uncomfortable feelings or tension. Who could I turn to for advice?

The next day I went to visit my swami at the temple just off the Cape. I had been involved in Hinduism for several years, first visiting the swami at the Boston temple and then recently at the summer temple on the Cape. I cried for a solid hour on the way, confused as to whether I should forgive an arguably minor transgression or end the marriage. I was sure the swami would say to forgive him, as most Western religions probably would. But, how could I?

As we strolled the grounds of the temple, Swami Tygananda said "You should end the relationship immediately."

What?! I could not believe what I was hearing.

"You have a lot more opportunities in the United States than in India. The rules about marriage here are more accepting of divorce and Carlos obviously has a bad character. Better to end it and move on."

"Um, okay... I'm going to think about that," I said. Now, my mind was completely blown. I had planned to stop by my friend Robbin's house on the way home, and as I drove images of Carlos and the girl swirled around with questions about forgiveness, character and the future.

I just want to get to Robbin's house, I thought. But, as I drove along the canal, I couldn't quite seem to find the turn. Tears of confusion and pain streamed down my face as I searched. *This doesn't even look like the right road,* I thought. I was making a u-turn when I saw the silver sedan heading straight at me. I let out a little scream as I braced for the impact.

I heard the car crash into my door and my head bounced off the windshield. My little truck spun completely around. I struggled to get my bearings. I seemed to be in one piece. I tried the door latch, but the door wouldn't open. I crawled out the passenger side of the truck. The driver, a guy in his thirties, came and sat with me as we waited for the police to arrive. We exchanged insurance information and his wife arrived. I overheard him say that his car was only two weeks old.

As we sat with the police officer explaining what happened, I heard myself saying "My huh, huh, huh, husband, ch, ch, ch, cheated on me..." and that's when the crying really started. Robbin's boyfriend, Matt, came and picked me up. After I was released from the hospital, I stayed at Robbin's house. Carlos arrived later and of course there was a tearful reunion.

Somehow, in that weakened state, I forgave him, at least initially but I didn't really trust him. And even after we moved to California so I could pursue my master's degree, I felt a certain amount of distance. I couldn't tell if it was my lack of trust or there was actually a reason to distrust him. *And why were there girls' cell phone numbers in his cell phone?* He always said it was me being paranoid - that he was a friendly guy and some of his friends were female.

It took three and a half years before I trusted him... and he promptly cheated on me again. I didn't want to divorce him. I believed in the sanctity of marriage and didn't want to end it frivolously. I thought of it as a personality issue relating to the way he was raised, but I couldn't even consider staying with someone I couldn't trust. After requesting the divorce from a judge, we walked out of the courtroom and I started crying. Carlos put his arms around me, saying that he was so sorry.

It took three years to wean myself away from him. We went back and forth and the whole thing was confusing, not only to me, but to my family as well. Once my parents came home and found us making out in the pool. *Ugh.* Eventually, I realized that spending that kind of time with him was not positive and I had to move on.

We were still friends technically. I felt responsible for him for some reason. Somewhere in my warped sense of values was a clause that says if you marry someone, you stay friends for life. After really separating from Carlos, I didn't date for a while, more by default than anything else. I didn't know what I wanted in a mate, and I was sort of fumbling around. I tried making lists of the qualities I was looking for and even joined a singles group. Nothing seemed to work. And then there was Bryan. *And now back to nothing. I have to get hold of my life.*

Chapter Three
28 Laws

The 28 Laws of Attraction are "highly effective principles, linked together like facets of a diamond." The author, Thomas Leonard, was one of the first pioneers in the field of "life coaching," and the book is the compilation of his coaching wisdom. According to the author, you could start with any of the principles and reap great benefits. And yet when you focus on one principle you see that it is linked to several others. I worked diligently on the various principles in an effort to improve my life, but the 28 Laws weren't a road map by any means. They were more like a To Do List... or more precisely a Super To Do List - each principle contains about a zillion things to work on.

The basis of the 28 Laws of Attraction is "Selfishness." However, it is not "selfishness" in the way one might think. The first principle is to "Become Incredibly Selfish," and when I first read it, I was a bit put off. I'd devoted my entire professional life in the nonprofit sector to helping people, both known and unknown. How could I possibly embrace such a concept?

What I came to understand was that Selfishness as defined by Thomas Leonard doesn't mean what it seems to. According to Leonard, selfishness doesn't mean being pitiless or cold-hearted. It means taking care of yourself to the point that you are so strong and stable that you can easily care for others, without it detracting from your base. The idea is to fill up your own cup to the point that it runs over and that which runs over, you can then give to others. The book goes on to explain that people who build their identities on trying to "do good" all the time, are "drainers." It takes a lot of energy to fulfill their sense of self-worth. And where does that energy come from? The people they are supposedly serving. *Sounds familiar...*

In this way, Selfishness is not egocentricity or insensitivity, but more a way of creating boundaries and taking care of oneself. It is actually ultimately - selflessness. The book suggested that it would take practice, and one thing I had to practice was saying "no." At work, I would habitually take on more and more projects but I always delivered the same high level of quality, regardless of the increased stress. I could see that this was an area to work on.

In dealing with my family, it was difficult to say "no" to their requests. After reading The 28 Laws, I decided to start saying "no" without an explanation. When my mom called and asked me if I was attending my two year old nephew's birthday party, I said "No, I'm not." The last thing I wanted to do was spend an afternoon with a bunch of two-year olds. There was silence as she waited for an explanation.

"Well, why not?" she said finally.

"I'm just not," I said flatly.

"Well, I think you should consider..." *I don't owe her an explanation,* I thought.

"I'm just not going. Listen, I've got to go. Bye," I said and hung up the phone.

At first there was shock and surprise in response to this new strategy. People didn't know how to react. It felt liberating. I was kind of shocked myself. The world didn't end. People seemed to accept it. Still, I decided to use this new power sparingly.

The 28 Laws insisted that treating yourself well was actually a very powerful strategy. "The real value of becoming selfish is to give your gifts room to develop," wrote Leonard. I wasn't exactly sure what this meant, but I could see that my life had become so draining that I had little time left to develop any of my past or present gifts. *Do I even have any gifts?* I wondered. *Yeah, I can organize the hell out of a project. Hmmm...I don't think that's what he means by gifts...*

Leonard also suggested that it was necessary to take what you need, even if it seems that others won't get as much. That was hard to swallow. He went on to explain that as you become a more solid person and start getting what you need, others will understand the importance of taking what they need. They will feel better able to count on you when the chips are down. Leonard also underscored the importance of being clear about what you want in interactions.

I tried to be open to opportunities and "to over-respond immediately" as they arose. When I was at dinner with my sister I took an extra serving without stopping to think about it. It was time, I decided, that I started to get what I needed. When I was online looking for something on a website I saw an ad for a glamorous free vacation. I

31

immediately filled out the form. When I was offered the choice of magazine subscriptions I purchased two.

Another concept related to selfishness is "extreme self care." This involves taking care of every aspect of one's physical needs, as well as eliminating stress and making the home a restful and nurturing environment. Everything has to be organized and clean, with no clutter. This was tough because in my family things like order and cleanliness were never priorities.

I started to force myself to make the bed every day. Initially, I hated it. But fairly quickly I began to see the value. Every time I walked by the perfectly-made bed, I felt a quiet sense of satisfaction, as if everything was in order. I reorganized my home office, filing papers and clearing off the table for the first time in years. What was once a comfortable mess was becoming an orderly, harmonious space ready for me to create whatever I could dream up.

Step #15 of the 28 Laws of Attraction is to "Tolerate Nothing." The book defines "tolerations" as which that bug us, sap our energy and can be eliminated. Inherently, they drain away contentment and good fortune. When you put up with something that you shouldn't, you disrespect yourself. The more you tolerate intolerable things, the less attractive you are to yourself and others. I found that interesting. I wondered what I had been tolerating. Probably quite a few things, especially at work. I determined to keep an eye out for tolerations.

One of The 28 Laws that I had a hard time with was "Unhook Yourself from the Future," in which Leonard suggests that it is much more important to perfect the present than to live in a far-off future. When I first read that, I was like *Are you kidding?* For most of my life I had been focused on the future, trying to create some perfect end result. Granted, I have accomplished a lot, including several degrees and certifications, but the book was right. My head has been more in the future and I hadn't created a present that I enjoyed. The instruction was to give up goals that were seductive and focus on fixing the present. The future, said Leonard, is nothing but a seducer. According to him, "When the future becomes far more interesting than the present, the destination holds more importance than the journey."

I was going to have to get serious about fixing my life, in the present. Apparently, that included giving up television. I realized that I was spending way too much time watching TV. According to the author, TV was more or less a sedative, a pleasure provider in the short term, but a thief of the present moment. *Seriously*? After coming home, most nights I would fix something to eat and then settle in front of the TV flipping from channel to channel, sometimes watching two shows at once. *Oh, no. How could I give up TV?*

Another thing Leonard suggested was to stop overplanning. *Okay, now that is going TOO FAR.* "Planning" was my middle name. I had achieved every major accomplishment in my life because of my stellar planning abilities. I was currently responsible for submitting 40 grant requests and 10 reports annually, using a project management system that I had created and managing a consulting practice with 14 consultants on the side. I used time management and project management software to keep it all straight.

Am I going to become some loose, go with the flow, willow in the wind? I wondered. Actually, Leonard suggested that it's good to identify a vision or sketch out a new plan. But to evolve you must be willing to "hold the plan lightly." *Okay, I like that part. I can hold a plan lightly... Maybe there's hope.*

***

Over the first weeks of my experiment I tried to think of new activities to fill my time. I made a point to stop by the Bonita Center for the Arts in order to get their current class schedule. Art had always been in the background of my life. My dad was a painter and art was all around us, *literally*. He stopped trying to sell his art early on and our house was always filled with his paintings. Our living room was a constantly-changing art gallery.

As children, our drawing and coloring was encouraged as much as reading and writing, but my dad was "The Painter." After coming home from whatever marketing or sales job he currently had, he would entertain us with stories from his day, eat a quick meal, and then spend hours on end in his studio.

The only way I got to spend any one-on-one time with him was when I'd sit on the floor of his studio while he painted. I'm not sure why he would even let me in. I would hesitantly knock on his studio door and then creep in and watch quietly. Sometimes he was so absorbed in his painting that he didn't even notice me sitting there. Occasionally, he would show me some art techniques. He worked in oils, which seemed very important and mysterious. All of the masters worked with oil paint and he always stressed the importance of cleaning the brushes thoroughly after each use. Such discipline was in stark contrast to the chaos of the rest of the house.

Usually he would just talk to me about whatever philosophical or spiritual concept he was contemplating at the time. Sometimes he would not allow anyone in the studio for weeks on end. When he would finally put the last brush strokes to his creation he would excitedly usher my mother and me into the studio to view it. Even as a child I could see that his art was the work of a master painter, rivaling even the best of the masters: Picasso, Van Gogh, Rembrandt. His style was abstract, combining air brush and detailed brush work, uniquely his own.

Sometimes the content had adult aspects to it, so when he'd ask what I thought, my eleven-year-old brain would struggle with the inability to adequately appreciate it or express something meaningful. Often I ended up with the same critique: "It's very… interesting." I really wanted to appropriately appreciate his amazing creations. Unfortunately for my father, half of his audience lacked the vocabulary and maturity to appreciate his work.

In high school, I started embracing art as part of my identity and began dressing the way I thought an artist would dress. Suddenly, there was a reason that I was different. Instead of being invisible or weird, I was an artist. "Oh! She's an artist. That's why she's like that." People finally had a label for me that made sense to them.

I, on the other hand, was somewhat ambivalent about totally identifying with the "artist" label. To me, art was just a skill, like any other skill. It was something that came easily. Of course I could paint and draw well—my father was a painter, it was in my blood. I appreciated the fact that I could pick up the skill whenever I wanted to but I wondered why I never had the urge to draw or the driving need to create, like my father.

Over the years I had done a few paintings, somehow overcoming the crushing intimidation of having a master painter for a father. However, it seemed like inspiration was rare. When I completed a painting, I was always extremely pleased. But it would be a long time before I felt like painting again.

Now, having motivation or not, I was going to take a painting class. I needed to fill up my time and this was as good a use of it as any. Perhaps by getting in the habit of painting, I would somehow overcome the inertia.

The Center for the Arts campus consisted of a series of creamy yellow, cottage-like buildings with white trim, connected by walkways. In the lobby of the main building, I requested their catalog of classes.

"Good afternoon. What can I do for you dear?" said an older woman at the front desk. She was wearing a peach-colored sweater set and had a pair of reading glasses hanging from a chain around her neck.

"Hi. Could you tell me about the painting classes?" I asked, looking around the empty lobby.

"Yes. Grab that schedule on the rack," she said. I handed it to her and she flipped through the pages. "Here are the painting classes. Page 25."

"Hmmm..." I said, looking through the brochure. The painting classes all seemed to be held during the day and cost several hundred dollars. *How am I going to be able to afford that?* I thought. "Do you have any classes at night?"

"Well, we have a drop-in class on Thursday evenings."

"That sounds good. How much is that?"

"It's $18 for two hours."

"Do you have to commit to a certain number of weeks?"

"No, just come by whenever you like, dear."

No commitment. No big up-front fee. Just come by whenever you like. My kind of class! "What level of students are in the drop-in class?"

"Oh, I'll have to ask the director about that..."

"Okay."

"Just a moment," She said, picking up the phone.

Jamie Sand, the director of programs, arrived a few minutes later. Jamie appeared to be in his early fifties with thick, sandy hair and a rumpled, button-down shirt. He described the various classes and agreed that the drop-in painting class would be a good fit for someone working full-time. Most of their classes were during the day.

"Would you like a tour of the campus?" He asked with a small smile.

"That would be great. Thanks."

The campus was nearly empty at that time of day. Walking through the quiet buildings I felt quite at home.

"This building is for dance," he said as we passed a door that lead to a large, open room.

"This room is for painting and sculpture," he said opening the door to a room that was filled with clay items. There were a few easels scattered about. *What if I'm not as good as the other artists?* I thought. "Jamie, what level are the other students?"

"Oh, there are all different levels. We haven't been getting a lot of people recently, just a handful. I teach the Thursday drop-in class," he said.

It did seem like a very laid-back, safe environment. I could picture myself in there taking a class with Jamie and some other artists.

"Cool," I said stepping outside. "Thank you so much, Jamie. I'm really looking forward to it."

"So, I'll see you on Thursday?" he asked.

"Um, I think so... probably. Thanks again." I felt very positive about the Center for the Arts. *At least one of my evenings is covered ... and it might even be fun.*

***

Journal Entry: 10-11-2013

I'm starting to feel better. I haven't felt as lonely and I'm looking forward to the art class on Thursday. My old friend Maria contacted me on Facebook. I was so surprised to hear from her. Really looking forward to lunch at her house.

Chapter Four
Business

At this point I had been in business for myself for almost two years, and it consumed all of my focus. Becoming a small business owner was never one of my goals, but a series of events led me to it.

I had been working in nonprofit management for close to five years before deciding to go out on my own as a consultant. I started out in my last organization writing grants and worked my way up to manager of program planning and evaluation, eventually becoming the organization's first chief program officer. When the recession hit I was demoted from chief program officer back to coordinating only grants again.

I was insulted that the organization didn't see the tremendous value I added in my former position, but I also understood that the director probably had to fight to keep me in the midst of budget cuts. I hated handling grants five days a week. I had decided that if I was going to handle grants for them, I might as well handle them for other organizations as well - as a consultant. The organization agreed to become my client and I managed their grant program three days a week. The other two days I worked on my developing my own business. Because of my strong time-management skills, I was able to provide the same level of output for them in three days as I had in five.

The president and the vice president of the organization were two of the most diplomatic people I had ever met. They knew how to handle virtually every situation that arose, no matter how delicate, difficult or unpleasant. Just watching them over the years and seeing how they interacted with people changed me from being brash and rough around the edges to a smooth, polished professional.

But all that diplomacy came at a price for both me and the organization. People didn't say what they really felt and there was a heavy air of dysfunction that became oppressive. I started to see all the little things that I had been tolerating, like veiled insults and tiny power plays. One thing I knew about myself was that I needed variety. Sitting behind a desk, staring at a computer eight hours a day was beginning to get to me. So, I opened my own company.

I hired my sister Giselle to help me with the marketing. She was one of my inspirations. The second youngest of my sisters, she had overcome many odds to get to that point in her life. She had never attended high school; instead she partied and left school after the 9th grade. Following a particularly low point for her, I worked to help her start a new life, get a GED and begin college. While completing my master's degree, I tutored her in how to write papers and in basic math skills.

While she was in college her life took a series of twists and turns, including having two children. But her persistence paid off and she graduated the same year I started my company, with a bachelor's degree in business. I was completely impressed with how she had turned her life around and to this day I to hold her up as an example of transformation and triumph.

After graduating, Giselle needed experience and I needed marketing support. I asked her to come on board, part-time. We worked fairly well together. Since quitting high school she had worked a series of food service and retail jobs, which had usually ended with her quitting in huff after some real or perceived insult, which meant that she had to learn some basic business skills.

We talked almost every day on the phone and she worked on the marketing projects remotely. Over the course of a year and a half, she created a fantastic newsletter template, revamped my website, created a brochure, and numerous other tasks. However, I had to treat her with kid gloves to avoid her defensive outbursts. I measured my words as carefully a safety engineer in a nuclear power plant.

Because I couldn't offer Giselle a full-time position, I trained her to open her own business while she was working for me. I taught her how to interact with clients, time management, how to create invoices, etc. But it wasn't always easy. My needs had always taken a back seat to the needs of my younger siblings in my family and I often felt invisible growing up because of the amount of attention my parents paid to my sisters. I didn't realize it at the time; it was just part of my role in the family. Inevitably, some lingering resentment spilled over into my current relationship with Giselle. She would excitedly talk over me and I sometimes couldn't get a word in when we were speaking. But it was great to have someone on my team and I felt like she had my back.

I also hired an assistant to help keep me focused on high-priority tasks and appointments. Mary was a former administrative assistant who had decided to work from home after having her first child. She kept track of my schedule, booked my appointments, and generally kept everything running smoothly. She was a real problem solver with excellent computer skills. She was able to jump in and learn a new type of software in minutes. Mary was my right hand and Giselle was my left, although I hardly ever saw either one of them. I ran the business out of my house and both of them worked remotely.

The visibility of the company was growing and I was getting busier and busier. I developed a team of consultants to work with me, with each one specializing in an essential area needed by nonprofits, like fundraising, bookkeeping and marketing. Eventually, the team grew to 15 members. We helped nonprofits grow from fledgling start-ups to major players in the social sector. Revenue from the initial contract with my former employer kept things afloat, but meant that I had to run an entire company on two days a week.

Starting the experiment seemed to add stress in a way. Initially, I was in a good mood, but it was rapidly deteriorating as I noticed how much I had been tolerating. My weeks were so full. Every single hour of every single day was accounted for. Mary helped me jam as many appointments as I could into Tuesdays and Thursdays. On these days, I met with current or prospective clients and managed the projects. Everything was very carefully orchestrated.

***

On a particular Thursday, Giselle and I met up for a phone conference with a client named Jim, who was located an hour away. We were getting a little desperate for meeting space and we scheduled the call to take place from another client's building, following a meeting. After deciding that the lobby was a bit too open, we settled on the deserted lunch room in the back of the building. I was a little uncomfortable, worrying that some random person might walk in during the call, but, it had to be done.

I had rehearsed the call in my head several times, never finding a great way to deal with the fact that Jim was not keeping his end of the agreement, and that it was costing us money. We had gotten along very well initially, but over the last two months it seemed that we were his last priority. Jim had cancelled a meeting and then a phone call at the last minute. I had driven across town to be with Giselle for that call, only to have it cancelled. And the project was way behind schedule. Every time I thought about it my breath would get caught in my chest and my cheeks would flush.

Giselle and I were sitting at a round metal table with the cell phone between us.

"What are you going to say?" she asked.

"I'm just going to explain that we can't possibly work this way."

At the agreed-upon time, Jim answered the phone. He indicated that his assistant was with him and that we were on speaker phone.

This is it. I have to lay it all out. "Jim, as you know, the project is behind schedule and we are still waiting on text and photos from you."

"Yes, Geva. I know," he said politely. "Unfortunately, we've been delayed by other projects." Jim was a former attorney and used to arguing cases. *Not the ideal background for a nonprofit manager.*

"I realize you have other priorities, as do I, but frankly your delays are costing us money." *Did I really just say that?* I thought.

"I don't see how delays on our end could cost you money," he replied harshly. "We're the ones with a schedule."

I could feel heat climbing up my neck. *Doesn't he understand that time is money?*

Just then, his assistant Lily chimed in, "We've given you everything you've requested."

By now I was leaning over the phone and my voice was rising, "Lily, we gave you a list of the missing pieces weeks ago and haven't received anything yet."

"I--, I --, I don't think I received a list..." Lily said, sheepishly.

Giselle's eyes were getting very wide. We were usually very diplomatic and deferential with clients.

I continued. "Look, we only take on a limited number of clients in order to provide the highest quality service, and because of that we have very clearly delineated project timelines." I backed away from the phone a little as I went on. "Over the last month, you've canceled both a meeting and a phone call that I had specifically set aside time for."

Jim spoke up. "Geva, I do apologize for that inconvenience." He then turned his attention to Lily and added, "Lily, please make sure you provide Geva with the missing information." Then he turned back to me and stated icily, "Geva, we will do our best to keep to the timeframe."

With that, we all agreed to end the call and hung up.

Giselle and I sat in silence.

"That went well," she said grimly, looking a little stunned.

I was disappointed that I hadn't found a diplomatic, feel-good way to deal with the call, but I was also proud of myself for saying what needed to be said. *No more tolerations,* I thought.

That evening, I came across an article called "Preventing Burnout" by Melinda Smith, M.A., Jeanne Segal, Ph.D., and Robert Segal, M.A. on a website called HelpGuide.org. It seemed that I had a lot of the symptoms. According to the article, "Burnout is a state of emotional, mental, and physical exhaustion caused by excessive and prolonged stress. It occurs when you feel overwhelmed and unable to meet constant demands.

As the stress continues, you begin to lose the interest or motivation that led you to take on a certain role in the first place. Burnout reduces your productivity and saps your energy, leaving you feeling increasingly helpless, hopeless, cynical, and resentful. Eventually, you may feel like you have nothing more to give." Well, that sounded familiar.

The article went on to provide the following checklist of symptoms.

You may be on the road to burnout if:

- **Every day is a bad day**. *Well, I couldn't say that every day was a bad day, but certainly quite a few were.*

- **Caring about your work or home life seems like a total waste of energy.** *What home life? Everything is about work, and even there I'm losing interest.*

- **You're exhausted all the time.** *I am definitely exhausted. I have no energy for anything. I feel like I am running on adrenalin most of the time, winding myself up for a hectic day of work and then collapsing on the couch at night.*

- **The majority of your day is spent on tasks you find either mind-numbingly dull or overwhelming.** *Doing grants is definitely becoming mind-numbing. It's just one after the other. We don't even stop to celebrate when a grant is funded. Just on to the next. And they're all starting to seem the same.*

- **You feel like nothing you do makes a difference or is appreciated.** *It feels like an up-hill battle all of the time. After years of trying to improve southwest Florida hardly anything has changed. There are still people out of work and hungry. The only thing that has changed is that I'm really tired.*

***

Journal Entry 10-20-2011

I've been feeling very down and confused lately. I haven't been enjoying my work and I'm trying to figure out what direction to go in and what changes to make. Today I feel okay, probably because I have nothing scheduled. I'm just taking it easy.

It's only been a few weeks, but I can see a noticeable reduction in the amount of time I spend thinking about men. So that's a good thing. But I'm still so tired...

Chapter Five
A Super Reserve

Occasionally Bryan would come to mind, especially when I was hungry or tired, which I thought was interesting. *Why does that happen? Am I more vulnerable or needy when I am hungry or tired?* Sometimes I would think of him before I went to sleep at night. Just for a moment I would wish he was there to put his arms around me.

I had never met a police officer before Bryan and at the beginning was sure that we wouldn't have enough in common to sustain any kind of a relationship. Our first date was a concert. My sister had set me up with him. One thing that struck me, while sitting in the bleachers of the stadium, was how profoundly comfortable I felt with this complete stranger. I thought *That's odd. My nerves are usually on edge when sitting next to a strange man.* But, with him I was totally relaxed.

Everything was easy with Bryan. He was adventurous and ready for anything. On the weekends we explored southwest Florida, visiting aquariums, attending baseball games, or just lying on the beach. Most importantly, he was very affectionate and enjoyed kissing for no reason.

We were compatible in so many ways, but incompatible in the most fundamental ones, such as how we envisioned our lives. When I asked him how he saw his life in five years, his response was "Pretty much the way it is now." Aside from the fact that I was pretty sure I wanted a family, this apathetic stagnation was completely unacceptable to me. I use visualization constantly, both personally and professionally and I could hardly stand it when I heard his response.

I definitely wanted a man with goals and dreams. A man who didn't want a family was the deal breaker.

***

I wanted to take back my life and I wanted to be less needy. So, I decided to focus on my reserves. One of the most impactful chapters in the 28 Laws of Attraction was the one on creating a "super reserve," in which Leonard wrote about the need to get beyond a scarcity mentality. He suggested that that most people are accustomed to just getting by in life and are prone to "scarcity-based worrying."

When I first read that, I instantly identified with it. My family had always struggled to get by and although I had put a little money into stocks, there were many areas of my life that were insufficient. I still viewed life with a scarcity mentality. Simply stated, the author felt that having enough to "get by" is simply not good enough. It is necessary to go beyond "getting by," to achieve the state of having more than what is needed of certain essential things, in other words - a super reserve. "You don't want to be greedy and you don't want to be needy," Leonard writes, "You just want to be so well supplied, that you will be able to lead a terrific life."

Apparently, a reserve can be in any area, material and nonmaterial. In the book, there was a seven-page checklist separated into categories, which covers home and comfort, car, financial, safety, energy, opportunities, space/time, calamity protection, supplies and relationships. I didn't do too badly, but the checklist gave me quite a bit of food for thought. There were plenty of areas in which I needed to improve. I didn't have a very strong base of operation, either tangible or intangible. My house wasn't as comfortable as it could be and didn't really reflect my style. It was pre-furnished when I moved in. I hadn't changed much. Financially, I wasn't in a strong position. My energy wasn't as high as it could be either.

Leonard instructed readers to pick one easy area that could be fulfilled immediately and I promptly went out and purchased a year's supply of toilet paper and laundry detergent. Next, I bought a safety kit for the trunk of the car, which came in a cute, little red duffle bag filled with flares, a blanket, and all kinds of things. I remembered feeling a certain satisfaction in arranging the huge plastic detergent bottles on the shelf behind the washing machine and dryer. I bought a new comforter for the bedroom, which brightened things up. I started de-cluttering the home office. I even bought shelves for the garage to use for my new reserves.

The space/time category was interesting. Leonard asked if you arrive early for appointments and if you promise less than you can deliver. "Personal needs that are not met are an insidious drain," according to Leonard. He also asked if you maintain extra time in your schedule or if you "over-book." I failed miserably in the over-booking area. I usually rush from one appointment to the next. I didn't do so well in the relationship category either, unsurprisingly. My emotional needs were not "more than met by my family, friends and colleagues." I actually failed seven out of ten of the questions. *Note to self: start building a super reserve.*

Chapter Six
Yoga Festival

"Mom, I've decided to take this year off from dating." We were in my parents' kitchen and my mom was putting the dishes away.

"Really?" she said, barely concealing her disappointment.

"Yes, I want to focus on my life for a while."

"Well, why a whole year? Can't you just take a few months off? You know I met a guy recently that I think you'd really be interested in..."

"No mom, I'm serious. I want to completely change my life and I think it'll take a year." She looked down, crestfallen. My mother had been after me since I was 21 to get married and have children. The expression on her face indicated that she thought I was stalling again.

"Hmmm... What do you mean exactly by change your life?" she asked.

"Well, I think I should make it more fulfilling so that I'm not so reliant on men. It's not very attractive you know, to be needy. I'm thinking of taking an art class and who knows what else."

"Well, honey you might need this then," she said handing me a spiritual magazine. The magazine listed events, mostly north of us in the Sarasota area. I usually ignored that particular magazine, being something of a spiritual snob. It seemed kind of flakey and new agey, with articles on everything from angel visitations to the power of pet psychics. But I remembered to open myself up to new things and while browsing through it, I came across an advertisement for a yoga festival in St. Petersburg.

I wonder what a yoga festival is like. The first time I did yoga I was six years old. I remember my dad doing a "sun salutation" in my parent's bedroom with the morning sun actually coming through the window. I tried to copy him as he stretched out flat in plank position and then came up to standing with his hands in prayer position. I also remember another time when I was sitting next to my mom while she tried to meditate and my little sister squirmed impatiently on the other side.

I started practicing yoga in 1993 when I went to the Kripalu Center in Western Massachusetts for rest and relaxation. The yoga was okay but it still wasn't really my thing. I think I enjoyed the rest and relaxation more. Over the years, I went to Kripalu occasionally whenever I need to get away and re-center.

Because yoga had always been in the background of my life, I never focused on it too much. For me it was a way to wring a little stress out of my body. I didn't think of it as a spiritual practice, so much as a relaxation practice. In 1998, when I graduated with a degree in biochemistry (which I had no idea what to do with) I turned to Kripalu. For me, their Spiritual Lifestyle Program (SLP) seemed like the next logical step. I spent three of the best months of my life there.

Kripalu is former monastery which was turned into an ashram and then became a yoga center. Despite the fact that structurally it was a cross between an office building and a hospital; to me it felt like a big, warm cocoon. My troubles and anxieties would begin to melt away as soon as I drove past the wide lawns and wildflowers that lined the long, meandering driveway.

Each group of "SLPs", as we were known, was named according to the month they arrived. My "October family" was made up of eleven fairly varied individuals. They were mostly open-minded, laid back people who wanted to hang out and do yoga for three months and maybe advance a little spiritually.

Over the course of the three-month program, everyone else would get up at 6 am and do yoga. I, of course, would sleep in. Then we would do "seva," or selfless service in whatever area we had been assigned to. I was in the housekeeping group and our seva consisted of making a lot of beds and vacuuming a maze of hallways. There was a precise way of doing every task, including vacuuming.

"Why do we have to follow straight lines and make a grid? What difference does it make?" I asked the team leader.

"We want you to get used to doing things consciously. Even seva is part of your program." That made sense to me. I liked the idea that while I was vacuuming, I was also practicing being conscious.

We attended small classes on spirituality weekly and explored our feelings in endless "sharing" groups, which I loved. Gathered in a circle, participants would talk about whatever was going on for them and how they were feeling. The rest of the group would sit and receive them without commenting or responding. I took full advantage of that process and enjoyed being listened to in such a safe environment.

In the mornings, before seva, we would assemble for a quick sharing circle. Sitting on cushions with backs propped against the wall we would share whatever was on our mind. Often, considering the early hour, the shares would sometimes be things like "I feel sleepy. I want to go back to bed."

At other times, they went a little deeper. "I miss my family; I haven't seen them in over a week." Many people who spent time at Kripalu brought heavy loads with them: depression, illness, loss. Those shares sounded more like "I have a heavy stone in my heart that just won't move."

I usually shared whatever came to mind in the morning sharing circles, but I saved my heavier and more serious shares for the weekly "family sharing circles." In the safety of my new, supportive family, I shared everything from my issues with men, my childhood, my family, and questions about the future. They listened with loving eyes and ears and accepted me, flaws and all.

In the afternoon, there was a second yoga class. This one I would attend. In the evenings we were allowed to join some of the activities offered to the public like chanting or musical performances. I was becoming intrigued with the spiritual concepts that I was learning and I wanted to know more. I searched through Kripalu's little library but couldn't find exactly the right book. I left the program and drove to the nearest town with a bookstore.

By some divine chance at a little, used-book shop in Great Barrington I encountered one of the most influential books of my life "Atmaboda," or Self-Knowledge, by Swami Nikhilananda. The book is an in-depth summary of Vedanta, the study of the ancient Indian texts called the Vedas. Everything Nikhilananda wrote made perfect sense to me. Hinduism, of which Vedanta is a part, is the only religion which allows a person to view "God" as either having a personality, like the traditional old man with a white beard or something vast and unknowable.

I tended toward the vast and unknowable viewpoint, but could understand the need to approach God by considering it to have a personality. And I thought it was both smart and intriguing that the original writers of the Vedas (a multitude of both male and female writers) would have the level of detachment necessary to realize that both viewpoints existed and that both were valid.

One thing that I liked about Vedanta was the concept of maya, which "veils the truth of our divine nature" and causes us to accept that which is false as real. And through our practices, we could eventually strip away this ignorance and become pure consciousness. I liked the fact that self-improvement was in my hands, rather than in the hands of a capricious or ill-tempered deity. Atmaboda so thoroughly and gracefully covered the essential concepts, that I was ultimately inspired me to accept Hinduism and Vedanta in particular as my chosen religion.

I collected the new concepts like beads on a necklace that I was slowly crafting at Kripalu. I wanted to savor every experience, every change. And SLP coincided with almost all the major holidays that year, including Halloween, Thanksgiving, Christmas and the New Year. Over that three month period, our October family became very close. My "sisters and brothers" commented on how my rigidity had crumbled, and how a new and softer, person had emerged.

When the three months were up, it was actually heart-wrenching to think of life without that huge, supportive family. On the last day of the program, we built a small bonfire out in the snow. One of my "sisters" beat slowly on a disc-shaped drum with a wooden mallet. We all chanted and placed our "intentions" (written on little pieces of paper) into the fire.

The advertisement for the St. Pete Yoga Festival had a smiling elephant holding a lotus. It looked like a lot of fun. Maybe I could get back some of that Kripalu magic despite being 1,200 miles away. With five events over three days, I knew I wanted to attend, even though it was two and a half hours away. My assistant Mary, helped arrange all the logistics, including the lodging. When registering, I tried to decide which events to sign up for. After figuring out the cost of various combinations, I remembered the Law of Attraction about over-responding and purchased the weekend pass.

The drive up was relaxing. As I headed north, I could feel my cares lessening with each mile. As I neared my destination, I wondered what the weekend would bring. I wondered what the "La Verandah Inn" was like. It sounded so cool from the description, and in the pictures it looked like a tropical oasis. The website showed a two-story colonial house with a big porch, surrounded by palm trees.

It had been such a long time since I'd had any time off, and I badly needed this break. I had secretly prided myself on never taking a vacation in five years, not counting the long weekend in Puerto Rico. *Why had I done that? No one cared whether I took a vacation or not...* No one was impressed with that, not even the people I worked with!

I had to drive around the block a few times before I spotted the entrance to the Bed and Breakfast. Driving into the little parking area, I noted lots of potted plants lining the entrance and a long staircase leading to the second floor. An extended porch wrapped around the front of the building and I wondered if the innkeeper would be around, considering how late I was arriving. It was already early evening. The woman I had spoken to had indicated that she would be there for most of the day.

As I approached the steps, I noticed a little basket with envelopes in it. *Interesting…* I thought as I went up the steps. A door with a sign that said "office" was to my right. I knocked. No answer. *Great. Now what?* Long purple and green glass wind chimes tinkled in the afternoon breeze. Empty tables and chairs lined the porch. I had a moment of panic, wondering what to do next. I hoped one of those envelopes were for me.

I checked, and indeed there was an envelope with my name on it and a key inside. Sighing with relief, I made my way to the stairs. By the process of elimination, I determined that the first room on the second floor was mine. I hauled my suitcase inside, surprised at the cozy sitting room. This led to a bedroom on one side and a bathroom on the other. There were pretty Victorian decorations throughout. *What a nice base for my weekend adventure!*

I checked the schedule I had printed out for the time of the first event, a concert at the Unity Church. I had a little over an hour to eat and find the church. I managed to find a burrito joint on the way. As I ate, I wondered what kind of people would be at the event. When I arrived, people were already filing into the church. Everyone seemed to be in a hurry. Inside, I took a seat on the end of a middle aisle. A guitar player named Jim Beckwith was joined by a bass player and African drummer on stage. Beckwith's songs were soulful and accompanied by an upbeat mix of world music. It seemed like a good sign for the weekend.

There was something familiar about the singer. He reminded me of someone and I couldn't quite remember whom. Maybe my first boyfriend Jason, with whom he shared a sweetly aloof quality. At the break I purchased one of Beckwith's cds. *Hmmm, he seems so deep. I wonder what he's like... Geez, will it ever end? I'm on a spiritual vacation and I develop a crush...*

After the break, a woman in white with long, blond flowing hair talked about the weekend, indicating that it was the first St. Pete Yoga Festival and that in addition to having five events, it was a benefit for the AMMA organization. She then introduced her husband who wore a long white tunic, white pants, and a crocheted white skull cap over his dark curly hair. He told us about the AMMA organization, named for a famous guru named Amma.

"Mata Amritananamay is known throughout the world as Amma, or Mother, for her selfless love and compassion," he said. "Amma has literally embraced more than 32 million people. She is known as the *hugging guru* and her organization also called AMMA has helped millions of people around the world with education, housing, and disaster relief."

The man in white then started a video on a big screen at the front of the church. There were pictures of Amma, a plump, Indian woman of indeterminate age with smiling eyes. She seemed to be everywhere, starting major projects, quickly changing lives. Having been in the social service sector, I marveled at the numbers of people whose lives she impacted and the breadth of her projects. She even donated funds after the Hurricane Katrina disaster in the United States. *How have I not heard of this woman before?*

The next morning, I sleepily greeted the innkeeper and she apologized for her absence the night before. I had registered under the special "artist rate," and she asked me what my medium was. "Acrylic and photography," I said guiltily. I hardly ever painted and didn't even own a proper camera at that time. "Um, yes... Acrylic. I paint with acrylic paints... and I love photography..." *Note to self: start actually making art, before you call yourself an "artist".*

I had breakfast at a table on the end of the wrap-around porch. While eating, I couldn't help but notice two squirrels running around some tree branches about 30 feet above my head. Suddenly, one squirrel jumped on the other, and there was some squawking. *Great,* I thought, *just what I need to see first thing in the morning - squirrels having sex.* I was even more surprised when one of them fell straight down and landed with a thud. It got up and slowly scampered away... *Lovely.*

I went back to the room, wondering if I really had the energy for an all-day workshop. *I'm so tired and this is the first time I don't actually have to do anything.* The workshop probably wouldn't be any good anyway. *Maybe I should just go back to sleep?* I decided to write in my journal out on the verandah and then see how I felt.

The empty verandah was breezy and cool. I kept thinking about the singer, Jim Beckwith. *Why, why, why? Why do I keep thinking about men?* I wondered about his soulful songs. He sounded so lonely. And he was so talented. As I wrote I realized there wasn't another event until the evening. *But, the workshop will probably be lame,* I thought. *Well, why not? I can always come back if it's no good. And it's got to be better than sitting around, thinking about a guy I don't even know.* I packed my gear and headed out.

When I checked in at the workshop I was given a special bronze necklace with the elephant god Ganesh etched on the circular disc as a gift for having purchased the full, weekend package. I grabbed a cushion from the pile on the wall and picked a spot. About 40 people were sitting in rows on the wood floor. Most of the attendees were wearing white yoga clothes or sweats. *Why did I wear this back blouse and leggings?* Eventually, a man with a beard and dark, curly hair and a white, crocheted cap took his place on the raised platform at the front of the room. I realized that it was the same man who had introduced the video the night before.

He introduced himself as Ram Gian and talked about how he had come to Kundalini yoga. "During a particularly troubling time in my life a few years back, my wife, Vananda convinced me to accompany her to a concert at the Unity Church in Clearwater," he began. "I have a motto, one I learned the hard way: 'Happy wife, happy life' So, I went."

We all chuckled.

"During the intermission, about 300 women assembled in the lobby waiting for their turn in the restroom. Suddenly, I spotted a crazy-looking guy in white with a long, black beard, and a turban. Armed with a short, but potentially deadly sword (should he unsheathe it), he fought his way through the women." Ram Gian paused and leaned back on the platform.

"Then, I realized, tipped off by the unblinking focus of his dark eyes on me, that I represented his ultimate destination. Being from Brooklyn and having had not a few such unprovoked confrontations, I braced for a fight.

61

Instead, on arrival, he handed me a flyer for Kundalini Yoga Teacher Training at Yoga Village."

"Huh?" he said quizzically, before continuing. "Then, the strange and knowing Sikh turned and disappeared into the sea of faces. But ever since that night, thanks to my wife, I practice Kundalini Yoga as taught by Yogi Bhajan" He brought his hands together and wrapped them around his knees. "And it takes me inside, to the Kingdom of Heaven within every time."

Ram Gian went on to explain that Kundalini yoga saved his life, allowing him to deal with the abuse and pain that had plagued him since childhood.

Over the course of the day, Ram Gian shared concepts derived from both Kundalini yoga and Advaita Vedanta, which was a bit shocking to me. I had longed to come across someone who shared my interest in Vedanta. I had even tried unsuccessfully to start a local study group devoted to the subject, but, no one ever showed up. And here, Vedanta had found me on its own.

Ram Gian's discussion wove together concepts from science, religion and philosophy in a way that was very impactful. He talked about space and time, the purpose of life, and self-identity. I looked around and people were either crying or holding back tears. Before we broke for lunch, he asked people to write any questions they had on little pieces of paper and leave them up front. I wrote out three and put them on the platform.

After lunch we returned to our spots and I was surprised to find that Ram Gian had chosen my question to begin with. It was: "How do we choose the right people to bring into our lives? How do we avoid getting hurt?" His response was good, but, the part that struck me the most was when he said "Forgive people that have hurt you, for they know not what they do. " He put particular emphasis on the "for–they-know-not-what-they-do." That's when the tears started.

"People have very little control over what they do," Ram Gian stated. "They are programmed by their environment and by what has happened to them over the course of their lives. They can only act out that programming."

Tears were streaming down my cheeks and I had to lie down. I felt the weight of a million wounds I had been carrying around lifting from my shoulders. Ram Gian continued his talk, responding to the various questions on the little pieces of paper. As he spoke, I recognized long-forgotten concepts from Vedanta, such as the concept of unity or non-dualism, which he explained in such a way that resonated far more than reading it in my various Vedanta texts had done.

"There is no separation between God and people," Ram Gian said. "We are all pieces of God and together we make up God. There is no duality. Separation from God exists only in our minds."

Eventually, I uncurled from the little ball I had become on the floor. In the afternoon, Ram Gian guided us in some Kundalini yoga to open our energy channels. We raised our arms in quick upward movements and then alternated raising and lowering our legs one after the other. I had never done Kundalini yoga before, and while the rapid movements surprised me, the certainly woke me up. We closed with a prayer and headed off into the afternoon sunshine. I felt extremely grateful for the experience.

After resting at the Verandah, I returned to the Unity Church for a concert with Parvati, a famous performance artist in the yoga circles who had wild, medusa-like hair and colorful outfits. She had an extensive stage show and it didn't take long for me to realize that she was the same performer who had come to the Kripalu years ago. Her performance seemed stale, as if it hadn't changed much since the late 90s. I left early.

The next morning I got up and headed out to the Sunken Gardens, where there was a full day of yoga classes scheduled. The air was crisp and the grounds were filled with lush, tropical plants, both manicured and wild. People were milling around trying to find their classes. My bracelet gave me admission to any of the classes, so I chose one in an open area with a cement floor and trees all around.

The instructor said she was from the Gold's Gym in St. Pete. We went through the poses (or "asanas") but her instruction wasn't particularly inspiring or profound. In fact, it felt a bit mechanical, as if she was just having us do the poses with no connection to them. She didn't choose any interesting or challenging asanas, but, it *was* nice to be outside.

Afterward, I wandered around, ending up at a workshop called "Yogic Spirituality Demystified." I gleaned from the program that it was for yoga instructors, but thought I would check it out anyway. We sat on folding chairs under live oak trees and people discussed basic yoga topics.

There are six branches of yoga: hatha (physical), bhakti (devotional), jnana (philosophical), karma (service), raja (meditative) and tantric (ritual). Jnana was my path. Jnana (pronounced nahnuh) was the path for reaching God through philosophical study. All six paths are said to lead to enlightenment, but I knew that jnana was for me. I enjoyed Hatha yoga because I liked doing the poses and being active, but it never felt like the same sort of profound spiritual experience as meditating or studying scripture.

It was always frustrating to me that there was such a divide between the physical or "Hatha" yoga and the other branches of yoga. In the United States, Hatha yoga seemed so divorced from the deep spiritual concepts of its roots. It had become something that people did purely for exercise. At least this group was attempting to bridge that gap by trying to talk about the spiritual component, but, neither the leader nor the students had anything interesting to say. I fidgeted in the hard, folding chair and left after about 20 minutes.

That evening, there was a meditation workshop with a Bhuddist monk from Sri Lanka on healing through loving kindness. I took my place in a pew alongside a group of people who were chatting about the festival. The church was alive with conversation and movement. I noticed the singer Jim Beckwith, dressed all in white. He took a seat to my right, a few rows back. *Wow, he's into spirituality as well. Stop brain, stop!* I wrenched my attention back to the stage and tried to clear my mind.

Eventually, a small man with brown skin and a long, garnet-colored tunic sat down in a chair at the front of the stage. He had a gentleness that permeated the room. He introduced himself as Bhante Sujatha and explained that he had known that he wanted become a monk at a very early age.

He began, "Initially, my parents (who were both Buddhists) were not entirely thrilled about the idea of their young son becoming a monk. But, I persevered and eventually persuaded them this was my true desire, and when I turned 11, my parents finally granted me permission to enter the monastery."

"Compared to their American counterparts, life for young boys in Buddhist monasteries is quite rigid." Bhante continued. "The young monks were expected to rise at 4 a.m. and make tea for all the other members of the temple before beginning their chanting and meditation practice at 5 a.m. Only two meals a day were served at the temple: breakfast and a large lunch. After breakfast, we studied scriptures, followed by more chanting and study time. At 11 a.m., we showered and laundered our robes. Lunch was followed by five hours of study in the classroom, and at 5 p.m. it was time for a second round of temple cleaning. The entire day was scheduled."

"In addition to our study and meditation, we young monks were also expected to go into town and do alms collections. For this, we would carry bowls into which the townspeople donated food for the temple."

Bhante said the most important thing he learned at the monastery was "how to get along successfully with other people anywhere in the world." As a result of the rigorous training he completed in the monastery, he believes it is "much easier to handle other people (and their various issues and personalities) when you've learned how to handle your own."

After obtaining his permanent residency in the United States, Bhante decided it was time to do something different. Although he enjoyed spending time with the Sri Lankan community in the US, Bhante wanted to do something to help his fellow Americans, who he said always seemed "vaguely dissatisfied despite their many possessions and high standard of living" and that they were "constantly striving after the next best thing."

Bhante believes that he is not only teaching meditation, but also "teaching people how to be happy." He said that his primary goal is to help people apply the teachings of Buddhism to their everyday lives.

"I hope to help people here by teaching them to see their jobs and work as a form of spiritual practice," he told us. "Then they can learn to enjoy whatever they are doing in the moment, instead of always worrying about the future or the past. That's the most important thing."

Bhante further explained that, "for monks, meditation is a very different practice than for regular people living in a community. Since monks spend most of their time in a cloistered environment away from the rest of society, they do not face many of the same challenges as other people who must contend with family and relationship stresses, along with the intense pressures that career and daily life often entail."

He then talked about how, over time, his work began to focus on helping others to comprehend the concept of loving kindness. He gave several examples of people he had worked with, whose painful burdens had been lifted. He explained that when you forgive others it is actually a selfish act, because it frees you.

After a while, Bhante asked us to sit back and close our eyes.

"Clear your mind. Focus your mind on the body. Look objectively on the body.   "Relax. Feel sensations. Feel tensions. Relax. Your body can feel your thoughts. Your body responds to your thoughts. Your body communicates through sensations. Feel sensations. Relax."

"Feel the whole body with the mind. Relax. Pay attention to the body. Feel harmony with the body. Feel close to your self."

"Love is the most important practice. If we love ourselves it is much easier to love others. Love is not something that many people take the time to cultivate. For some loving kindness is something that may come easily. For others, it may take a lot of work. To give true love, one must start with themselves. After all, you cannot give what you do not have."

"Feel peaceful, loving thoughts for your self now. May I be well, happy and peaceful. Sometimes, if you observe your mind with clear awareness, you may find you have a lot of anger and hatred toward yourself. Ask yourself the question - 'why do I have hatred or anger toward myself?'"

"Maybe you want to control the world. Maybe your answer is - 'I cannot just do anything I want. I have to accept the way things are with gentleness and acceptance.' You can curb anger and hatred coming to your mind. Send your loving thoughts toward yourself. 'May I be well, happy, and peaceful."

"Focus your mind on your family, your parents, grandparents, brothers and sisters. Imagine their smiling faces. By name, send loving and compassionate thoughts towards them. Sometimes you don't like some family members, your brother or sister or parent. Ask the question - 'Why don't I like them?'"

"Sometimes, you want them to be the way you want. Maybe you want to control them. Perhaps sometimes they were rude to you, mean to you. Think - 'They are human beings like me. Forgive them.' Think - 'May they find happiness and joy in their lives. May all my family members be well, happy and peaceful.'"

"Now send your loving thoughts to friends next to you, behind you, all around you. May my friends be happy, well and peaceful."

"Now, send you loving thoughts to the whole world, all of the universe. May all beings experience peace. May all beings live in harmony."

"If you practice loving kindness meditation every day, every minute it can be a great remedy or healing power to heal you and others."

"May I be well, happy and peaceful."

I slowly opened my eyes. Looking around, I could see that everyone else was feeling as relaxed and contented as I was.

"Thank you for coming." Bhante said, closing his hands together in prayer position. "May you *all* be well, happy and peaceful."

On the drive home from the festival, I thought about the weekend's activities. Without question, the workshop with Ram Gian was the most impactful part. And I couldn't believe that I had almost missed it because I wanted to sleep in! The music had been inspiring as well. *Note to self: Need more good music.* And the monk's words were still with me. What a gentle soul...

***

Journal Entry: 10-30-11

Ever since the Yoga Festival, I have been trying to see God in every face. I've been doing this as a practice, as often as I can. When I see strangers on the street, I try to remember that they are God and I am God. There is no separation. Sometimes, it makes me smile and then they smile. People are so good to me in almost every interaction I have now.

I had a day in which I was happy all day. Sometimes I feel bubbly and happy. Sometimes I feel lonely.

I wanted to have a dinner party next weekend, but that's not going very well... can't get enough people interested.

I've been thinking of expanding my vision for the company, or maybe the boundaries of the company. I've been feeling like I haven't been able to make as much of an impact. I know I wouldn't even have had the space in my life to even come to these conclusions if I hadn't started the experiment.

Chapter Seven
Six Mile Cypress

November

I was determined to get out into nature, get more exercise, and spend more time alone. If I could start to enjoy being alone, perhaps I would be less needy in relationships. Thus, I headed for the Six Mile Cypress Preserve. I had never been to the Preserve and I didn't know what to expect. The Six Mile Cypress Slough (pronounced "slew") is a 2,500 acre wetland in Fort Myers, Florida, that measures approximately 9 miles long and 1/3 mile wide.

I had heard about it a million times due, to its interesting history. In 1976, a group of Lee County high school students who were studying the role of wetlands in Florida's ecology became alarmed at how fast these environmental treasures were disappearing, being swallowed up by private interests. The students, known as "The Monday Group" launched a daring campaign to save the area for future generations. They were eventually successful, convincing Lee County voters to increase their own taxes to purchase and convert the Slough into a preserve.

The road leading to the Preserve was undergoing tremendous construction, changing from two lanes to four.

The black top was being paved, with new lanes designated by cones and barrels. One would never guess that there was a nature preserve just on the other side of the trees.

As I turned into the parking lot of the Preserve, I entered a completely different world, serene and secluded. Pine trees shaded the parking spaces. I spent some time in the visitors' center, looking at all of the exhibits on the Preserve and southwest Florida habitats, trying not to compare them to the exhibits at the nature center where I used to work. The docent pointed out the boardwalk and suggested I visit it, since I was there.

Approaching the boardwalk, I noticed a family of five with an antsy toddler. I decided to let them go on ahead, slowing my steps. My shoes made soft clacking sounds on the boardwalk, and the sun was shining overhead. As people passed by, I tried to remember what Ram Gian had said about recognizing God in every face. An old woman came toward me and I looked into her eyes and smiled. She smiled back.

I entered the forested area, stepping into cool shade. The floor of the swamp was bare and dry with little Cypress "knees" poking up. I could hardly imagine the area filled with water after the summer rains. *I like this place. Why haven't I come here before?* It was beautiful. Mint-colored Lichens covered the railing in dry, lacey splotches.

I passed a wooden structure with bleachers, probably used for lectures by docents, who would describe the indigenous flora and fauna. The bleachers faced a cool, dark blue lake and I sat for a moment before moving on. Small groups passed by, often stopping for a moment to admire the lake. Everyone seemed to be in a hurry, including me. *Why can't I slow down?* I thought, as I walked on.

Bryan would have liked this place, I thought. We had visited a swamp in Naples once and I remembered that the beauty of the place combined with holding his hand had made me almost giddy. *Okay, that was then. This is now. And today is a beautiful day.*

After my walk, I returned to the car and pulled my black rollerblades out of the trunk. I strapped them on. They still looked new, with their futuristic molded plastic and straps that wrap across the front. In reality they were close to fifteen years old. The newer models looked more like sneakers with wheels on the bottom. New or old, at least they felt safe. My entire foot, heel and most of the shin covered.

I headed out to the road. Six Mile Cypress Preserve has a sidewalk which runs for miles along the side. Today, luckily the sidewalk was roped off, so I was protected from the chaos of construction. Rollerblading was unnerving with cars heading towards me. I felt very exposed, very much "on display". I picked up speed tried not to notice the cars going by. *This is my time,* I thought. *This is my experience.* A feeling of satisfaction filled me as I zoomed along.

***

Journal Entry 11-2-2011

Had dinner with Carlos last night, as friends of course. He spent the whole night talking about how much he missed his ex-girlfriend. I actually gave him advice. How bizarre.

The other day I received an email from a guy I had met years ago while kayaking. He asked if I would be attending an event coming up. It caught my attention a little, but not as much as it would have in the past. I replied in a friendly way, but remained resolved that I wouldn't get involved and would keep the vow.

In the 28 Laws of Attraction, Thomas Leonard insists that it is necessary to toss out every article of clothing that does not make you look great and that you must replace them with flattering clothes that you love. I got rid of a few things and bought a couple of fun skirts. They're soft and colorful and swish when I walk.

Chapter Eight
Happehatchee

It was 9:05 am and I was running late for yoga at the Happehatchee Center again. I tried to keep my heartbeat down as I zipped along, my yoga mat slung over my shoulder bouncing against my back in time with my steps. I was trying to focus on the narrow dirt path, but kept getting distracted by the beauty of the setting. The trees framed the walkway and the sunlight was shining through the leaves. The air was cooler than it had been in months.

I passed the caretaker's trailer and pushed through the rickety gate. On my right were the abandoned remnants of a butterfly garden, It must have been beautiful once, but was now little more than a tangle of pots and scraggly plants. Up ahead some yoga students were standing in front of a large, wooden gazebo. *It figures,* I thought. The instructor was late again. I slowed my pace.

I greeted the other students and made my way up the wooden steps. The large, open, octagonal space was almost full. Leaving my shoes by the entrance, I took a spot in the center towards the right side. Lush vegetation surrounded the gazebo on all sides and the screens of the enclosure made me for a feel like I was in the jungle yet within a comfortable and airy structure. Bobbie Lee, the instructor, made her way to the podium at the front of the gazebo. She had her red hair pulled into a pony tail and was dressed in her usual black yoga outfit. The black kohl surrounding her eyes had been drawn into points, giving her an Egyptian appearance. She strapped on a head set and took her place front and center.

The "Fusion" class was Bobbie Lee's own combination of martial arts, yoga and Pilates, an intense workout set to an eclectic mix of music. My favorite part was the Chi Gung segment, which is a practice of aligning breath, movement, and awareness for healing and meditation. Bobbie Lee described how the different movements were derived from nature and animals, and she guided us in moving energy around with our arms first in big, looping, cloud-like movements, and then in rushing waves.

Next was martial arts. The intensity of it always surprised me after the peaceful Chi Gung. Bobbie had us doing knife strikes to our imagined opponent's eyes and elbow blows to invisible jaws. After that came the yoga section where we straightened and lengthened our bodies, followed by a cool down. A quiet "shavasana," ended the class with us lying on our backs and soaking in all of the movements.

The only sounds were birds chirping and wind blowing gently through the trees. Bobbie Lee dismissed the class with her traditional blessing for us to do the best we could for ourselves, our community, the planet and all living beings. We got up to leave and another class had already begun filing in. I headed back to the car and traded my yoga mat for my new art bag.

My intention was to spend some quality time with myself out in nature. I had decided I would paint outside, which seemed like a very cool thing to do. I headed down a dirt path, looking for a good place to set up. I decided to settle in the first spot that called to me and just draw

76

whatever was around me, rather than choosing a necessarily scenic spot.

When I was young, we lived in Pennsylvania. Sometimes we would take hikes through some woods near our house up to the waterfalls. I remember being surrounded by the quiet immensity of the forest as we moved through, single file. The gentle sound of insects buzzing filled the air and bright green ferns greeted me along the way. I always felt enveloped in the majesty of the forest, as if I were just another of its many creatures walking along.

What had happened to those days, when I felt a part of nature? Growing up, my mother had always kept huge gardens, filled with vegetables. She knew all of the names of the plants and would point them out us as she tended them. The Latin names would go in one ear and drop right out the other one. But, regardless she instilled in all of us a deep appreciation for plants and living things.

We had raspberry and blackberry bushes behind our house and my sister and I would head out with enamel buckets to search the thickets for berries. Returning, my bucket would be half full and Grae's would have about three berries in the bottom, her hands and face stained purple.

We spent entire days outside, playing in the fields or walking in the woods. But, gradually my life had become an indoor experience. Over the years with every mile of moving, and every change of circumstance my reality had become rooms, buildings and air conditioning. *What a stale existence,* I thought.

Now, after looking around Happehatchee I found a place that looked comfortable and set up my gear. I had never actually painted outside before. *I hope I have everything I need.* I pulled out the pad of paper. *Pencils or watercolors? Hmmm…. Both.* I looked for my water bottle and the plastic mixing palette. *I wish I brought a snack.*

Around me were long, spiky, green plants and a few ferns, nothing too interesting. However, a spider's web was stretched between two of the leaves. I decided to capture it on paper, or at least try. I began sketching, but started to get the itchy feeling that I was supposed to be somewhere else. I couldn't quite settle into the moment, but I kept going. *The point is to do it.*

I noticed that the leaves had yellow stripes along their edges and I added that to the picture. On closer inspection, the leaves revealed dark, green splotches along their spines. There was actually quite a bit of depth to the scene and I tried to remember how to portray it. *Is it dark in front that leads to more depth or dark in back? At least the ferns look good.*

Before, I knew it, the picture was complete. I looked around for something else to paint, but nothing caught my attention. *Okay, that's enough for one day.* I had been there less than an hour and I was already hungry and impatient to leave. *Well, it was a start. I spent time alone in nature and actually painted outside.*

I spent quite a bit of time at the Happehatchee Center. Two year's prior, I had conducted a women's workshop series in the main cottage. I had been reading about a lot of concepts related to personal growth and wanted to share what I learned. I also wanted to try out giving a workshop series, which I had never done before. I wasn't sure how giving a women's workshop fit into my life or future, but I liked the challenge of it.

I marketed the series through a women's meet-up site online and a diverse group of women attended. They came from all different religions and all different levels of spiritual and personal development. Debbie was extremely an intelligent administrative assistant in her thirties. Mary Lu wore glasses and had a sweet voice. Her enthusiasm for all things related to spiritual growth was infectious. Many of the women brought friends.

I charged only $10 per session, partly because I had absolutely no credentials in psychology and partly because I just wanted to get the workshop series off the ground. Looking back, I can see that in some ways, the "experiment" was a natural outgrowth of the workshop series, and of all of the personal growth work I had done over my lifetime.

I called the series "A Woman's Journey" and designed it around Abraham Maslow's hierarchy of needs. Each workshop focused on one of the levels in the pyramid: physical, safety, social, love/belonging, esteem and self-actualization and so on. We met every two weeks and I ended up adding additional topics like creating healthy boundaries, romantic relationships, self-esteem and visualization. I believe that a woman's journey is her unique struggle to understand all of these topics over the course of a lifetime.

I acted more as a guide than an expert. I shared as much as I knew on each of the subjects, but, really we all learned from each other. Although I had an outline for the discussions, the series was modeled somewhat on the "sharing circles" of Kripalu and generally focused on learning by communicating each person's feelings, ideas and stories. It felt really good to be able to express the concepts that I was learning and to hear what the other women thought.

I held the series during the winter, and the cottage was drafty and cold. I had to set up a little heater to keep us warm. The women pulled blankets over their laps and drank hot tea, while we talked and learned from each other. It seemed like everybody in the room was struggling with how to be happy and what role men played in their lives. It never occurred to any of us to take men out of the equation and to focus on our own lives. Men were just a given, it seemed.

Oddly enough, I had never previously participated in any group or experience that was specifically and only for women. On some level, I had never identified myself as part of the larger group of women of the world. Being a woman, for me, was an individual experience. So, to hear their stories and feel that connection of being part of a larger shared story, was very powerful. And to find myself, leading the process was both humbling and unnerving.

On the little response cards I handed out, the women said they looked forward to the workshops and especially the sense of community that it created in their lives. Toward the end of the series we walked a labyrinth that was in the back of the property. It was nice to see all the women silently focusing their minds as they walked the swirling path, outlined by shells and stones. The only sounds were the crunching of feet on the dirt path. The series ended when the group reached the top of the pyramid, self-actualization.

None of us had a very clear understanding of what self-actualization really meant. We agreed that it meant fulfilling one's ultimate potential, but that the end point should be self-determined and not imposed by society. But by the end of the series, I ended up with a lot of questions about what my real needs were and what I really wanted out of life. Ultimately, I think the series influenced my eventual break up with Bryan and the start of my company.

Because of all the changes in my life since then, I hadn't spent much time at Happehatchee in the two years since the workshop series ended. I still attended Bobbie Lee's yoga class on Saturdays, but had few opportunities to visit Happehatchee until Bobbie Lee invited me to an instructors' meeting. Bobbie Lee was on Happehatchee's board of directors and she wanted me to meet some of the board members at the meeting. She hoped that the board would hire me to help Happehatchee grow through my consulting practice.

At the meeting, I found myself sitting in the same cottage that I'd used for the workshop series two years before, now filled with yoga instructors, tai chi instructors and a few board members. They wanted to create more income and to make Happehatchee financially sustainable. During the course of discussion, I put forth the idea that Happehatchee needed to build a solid infrastructure, especially a fundraising system but it seemed to fall on deaf ears.

It was at that meeting that I first met Jeanie. She was sitting cross-legged on a couch on the other side of the room. Bobbie Lee introduced her as the new executive director and official drummer (whatever that meant.) She seemed kind of kooky and free spirited, with her tie-dyed shirt, and long, wild hair. She definitely didn't fit my view of what an executive director looked like. When it was her turn to speak I couldn't understand what she was trying to say. Her sentences didn't seem to connect, and I couldn't follow her logic. I thought, *Great, just what they need.*

A few weeks later I attended a drum circle at Happehatchee, held behind the cottage building, behind the pine trees. It was almost dark when I arrived, and the drumming had already begun. I could see light from the fire through the trees and the shapes of people sitting in beach chairs. I was a little nervous going to an event where I didn't know anyone. *How bad could it be?*

I had never attended a drum circle before, and I was a little anxious because I didn't know what to expect. I had seen a notice about it in Happehatchee's newsletter and it seemed like a good way to get out of the house and be around people. As I walked down the path toward the campfire, I could see that there were about 10 people sitting in little clusters, drumming away... not quite harmoniously, but somewhat enthusiastically.

I picked up a drum from the small collection at the entrance and made my way toward the other side of the circle. I took my middle seat of three empty chairs, but immediately realized that the smoke was blowing in my direction. I moved down a few seats. Looking around, there seemed to be quite a variety of people present, from the patently hippie types to an older couple and a few young families.

Jeanie came in with a dark-skinned man wearing cargo pants and Bob Marley tee-shirt. They took their places across from me. The drum I was holding had a round top, made of some kind of skin... *gross,* over a wooden base. The top was held down with cords that ran along the sides. I looked around and tried to copy the way the others were hitting their drums. I couldn't get the thing to make anything resembling music. *How did they do that? How did they make those patterns of sound? I am completely uncoordinated. This is never going to work.* I decided to just tap the thing over and over again. *Well, that's not too bad.*

I noticed a guy a few seats away wearing shorts and a tank top. His long legs were stretched out in front of him, and his tank top accentuated his tanned muscles. He had a little boy with him, and the boy kept squirming around in the seat. My mind began to wander, wondering if the man was single... *Wouldn't that be perfect,* I thought. *Stop it brain, stop. Come back to the drumming...*

After a few minutes, the drumming stopped and Jeanie stood up. "Hello everyone. Welcome to the sacred circle," she said looking around. "Please join me in an invocation. We will summon the energies of the four directions." She turned to the left and lifted her palms to the sky. "We offer prayers and blessings to the West, North, South and East and then a general prayer to create harmony." We faced each direction in turn and Jeanie offered a separate blessing for each.

We sat back down and the drumming resumed with some steady, gentle rhythms. I was still unable to copy even the simplest patterns, but Jeanie seemed to be an experienced drummer. She and the man with her were playing in sync, their hands moving rapidly over the drums in complicated patterns. *Why can't I do that? It doesn't sound the same.* I decided to play along by focusing on the main beat. Dah, dah, da... dah, dah, da.

It's nice to be outside, I thought. The fire crackled and glowed. More and more people trickled in over the course of a few hours and the energy of the drumming mixed with the energy of the fire. Dah, dah, da... Dah, dah, da. Rhythms came, built up, and passed away, replaced by new rhythms. *At least I can do the main beat*, I thought. After a while the energy started to wane and some people got up and left. The circle seemed to be petering out, so, I headed out as well, the drumming echoing in my mind... dah, dah, da... dah, dah, da.

***

Journal Entry: 11-5-2011

Well, I've had two good days in a row. It seems kind of hit or miss. Yesterday, I felt very relaxed, despite the fact that I had a workshop in the afternoon and had to give a presentation.

Maybe it's because I am adding space and time to my schedule. It might also be because I am trying to look at the experiment as adding to a base that I already have. I am adding to my life, not trying to create a completely new life out of nothing. The 28 Laws say to build on what you have.

Art class has been going well. My painting is coming along. It's a black and white scene of two high-heeled boots walking away. All you see are the boots, one in front of the other. It's at a tough point though. I have been painting all the details and now have to pull the shapes together. Jamie is a very patient teacher.

Chapter Nine
Pain of Growth

I had just arrived at the house and was considering what to make for lunch. I was famished. The skin on my arms was getting red, telling me that my blood sugar was plummeting. The phone rang. When I get that hungry I get irritable too, so I probably shouldn't have answered it, but I did.

It was my sister, returning my call about our plans to take my niece and nephew to the Nutcracker on the following weekend. I tried to explain that I had already spoken to my other sister and ruled out my nephew's participation. But, Giselle was speaking over me, as she often did, not listening. I had mentioned it to her several times.

Today, I couldn't stand it.

"I really think that it should just be the girls. Dalton will be bored and he'll complain..." Giselle said.

"Yes, I..." I tried to interject.

"He hates events like this and he wouldn't appreciate it..."

"Yes, but listen I..."

"I think everyone will be better off ..." Giselle kept talking, no matter how hard I tried to get a word in. I just wanted to say that I had decided against it but she wouldn't let me speak. Even though I was used to being talked over by her, this time it was really rubbing me the wrong way.

She kept going on and on about why Dalton shouldn't go. I couldn't breathe.

Finally I said "Will you shut up a second?"

"Well, you don't understand, Sasha..."

"Will you shut the fuck up?"

She started in again, and finally I screamed "WILL YOU JUST SHUT UP AND LISTEN?!"

Silence.

Then, she hung up.

Great. I totally felt like there was nothing I could have done differently, other than not answering the phone when I was hungry. I had no control over myself, but, on the other hand, it was like my "self" had finally come alive and would not be silenced by someone talking over it. I stewed about it for most of the weekend, and ended up writing Giselle an email that didn't exactly apologize. I didn't feel sorry for what I did, but I felt sorry for possibly ending my relationship with her. Of course, I didn't actually say that. I said something to the effect of being sorry that the situation had occurred, which was technically true.

The next few weeks were hard. Not only were Giselle and I sisters, but she worked for me. We worked together on a daily basis, communicating by phone and email. I had often felt like she was the only one "who had my back" and I think that kind of dependence may have contributed to my allowing her to speak over me from time to time without realizing it. *Apparently enough is enough. Boy, a lot of changes are taking place. What have I gotten myself into?*

***

Journal Entry: 11-20-2011

I haven't written for a while because I was waiting for something positive to report. I went through a period of time where for the most part I was okay, but not happy. One good thing I can say definitely is that the amount of time that I spend thinking about men has been greatly reduced. I still have a long way to go though.

This is actually a very hard time because I have ended friendships, and have not replaced them. I met someone who seemed cool, but turned out not to be. I've spent a lot of time alone. Sometimes I'm lonely. Not always, but sometimes. I am definitely getting better at being alone. When I started all of this, all I thought about was adding things to my life to improve it. I feel like I have been subtracting a lot. I went into this thinking about the positives. I didn't realize it was going to be hard at times.

Chapter Ten
Thanksgiving

When I arrived at my Mom's house for Thanksgiving, three cars were already in the driveway. I wondered what the evening would bring. I felt anxious as I walked up the path. Giselle and I hadn't spoken for two weeks, and I didn't know how things would go. Her car wasn't there yet.

Inside, my nephew Liam was running around in diapers, while my sister Garan chased him. My mom was in the kitchen working on dinner, and my dad was getting down a serving tray. I joined the work by setting the table, slowly positioning each piece in just the right place.

My sister Grae arrived, with her family. She headed to the kitchen to help my mom with the preparations. I used to take full responsibility for organizing the family events, even making charts showing who was coming and what everyone was bringing. Somehow I had lost interest in that. I just didn't want to be responsible for holding everything together. Within the last few years, I had taken on less and less responsibility until I was now just pulling my own weight at events instead of everyone else's as well.

Eventually, we were all seated around the dining room table. Dinner was about to begin when Giselle came through the front door, her arms filled with bags, Frankie and the kids behind her. I wasn't sure what to say, but, it didn't matter because she didn't even look at me. She said hello to everyone else, and breezed on out to the porch. Instead of crowding around the dining room table, she set her family up at the long table on the porch.

As our family kept growing, we had to keep trying different seating arrangements, but I couldn't help wondering if she didn't want to sit near me. The little group around the dining room table was lively and as usual focused on trying to get Dalton to eat. He always ate like a bird. I tried to join in the conversation going on around me, but felt disconnected and heavy.

I felt like there was something missing. For some reason, I felt very exposed, which is when it occurred to me - in the past, either Bryan or Carlos would have been there as a buffer between my family and me. This time I couldn't hide in a relationship or run from my feelings. This time it was me and them.

***

Journal Entry - 11-30-2011

I've had a few dreams in which handsome men are more interested in me than I am in them. This is a first. Most of the time there are no men in my dreams and if there are, the dreams are usually kind of anxious. But, this feels different. Maybe something is changing on a deep, fundamental level? During my waking hours, I hardly ever think of men or feel lonely anymore.

Chapter Eleven
Festival of Trees

December

It was Christmas time and my parents and I were headed up to the Festival of Trees at the Sydney and Berne Davis Art Center in Fort Myers. I had heard about the event, and invited them to come along. There was an antique car show in the street in front of the Art Center, and we decided to check it out first.

Vintage autos lined both sides of Main Street. The owners were sitting in lawn chairs on the sidewalk, in front of each of their cars. My dad was up ahead, checking out a 1959 Cadillac convertible, admiring the cherry-red finish. The double headlights and the shining front grille looked like a grinning set of teeth. My mother and I walked along the row of antique cars until we got to a 1955 Chevrolet Convertible with a red body and white top.

"Gene, do you remember this car? That was such a fun time…" she said, pausing. I was snapping pictures and my dad posed, arms crossed over his chest next to an orange, muscle car. The atmosphere was light and upbeat. People were milling around and enjoying the holiday spirit. Mom posed next to the Chevy and then the owner came over and insisted that she sit inside it for the photo.

It crossed my mind that this was probably the first time I had attended an event with my parents without any of my siblings along. *This is probably the first time that I've been unattached enough, psychologically, to have space to focus on being with them,* I thought. Prior to that, I was always either dating someone, wishing I was dating someone, or trying to date someone.

Not having my sisters and the entire extended family around made the awkward dynamic between me and my parents more obvious. The silence between us was more noticeable. Nothing had really changed. I was always a little quiet around my family, only speaking up if it was absolutely necessary, but here without the distraction of the other family members, the silence echoed between the three of us. We attempted to fill the space with small talk.

We arrived at the end of the row of cars, and made our way toward the Festival of Trees. Stepping inside, we entered a winter wonderland, with trees decorated in all different colors and styles, each one telling a different story. I saw a tree that I loved, covered with the giant red candies, and one decorated with the peace signs. Dad was especially fond of the tall tree made entirely out of teddy bears.

I came across a green and gold tree, decorated with Irish crosses and shamrocks, reminding me of my Irish grandmother. There was joy and excitement in the air as people admired the elaborate trees. Mom was wandering around, marveling at the trees, and drinking hot chocolate.

"Can you believe there are so many variations on the concept of a Christmas tree?" she said excitedly. Each tree had a small plaque with the name of the company that had decorated it. In a few weeks the trees would be auctioned off at a gala with the proceeds benefiting the Art Center.

The movie "It's a Wonderful Life" was being projected on a screen above a paper fireplace. Chairs were arranged in a semi-circle in front of the faux fireplace, and I sat down to watch. I thought about the meaning of Christmas. *Maybe it's about appreciating what you have and the people around you,* I thought. Dad sat down next to me.

"That's a great movie, isn't it?" he asked.

"I don't know," I replied. "I've never seen it before."

"Really?" He was surprised by my response. "Huh. I never knew that."

There's a lot you don't know about me, I thought.

***

Journal Entry: 12-15-2011

I miss Bryan. I don't want to think about him. I hope this experiment get easier.

Chapter Twelve
Christmas

I saw my family for Christmas but not Giselle. She took her family to Marco Island to spend Christmas with her husband's family, so there was no drama. We still hadn't talked.

I decided to buy myself a guitar for Christmas. I had wanted to play the guitar since I was very young. Even back then, I admired people who could just hang out with their guitars having fun. It looked like they didn't need anything else - they were in their own little world.

When I was six years old, my parents had gotten me a guitar and arranged for some lessons. But my little hands were so small that they barely fit around the guitar's neck. I couldn't make the notes and chords sound right. I think it was on the second lesson that I got so frustrated and quit. My parents didn't push it, and so that was that.

But, now I was older, my hands were bigger and I was far more determined. I bought the guitar from a shop on Rt 41. I had no idea what I was looking for, so, the owner suggested a starter guitar of good quality. He also gave me the number of an instructor who gave lessons in a little room in the back of the shop.

Derrick arranged to meet on Thursdays. The first lesson was pretty encouraging, but after making an appointment for the second lesson, he cancelled. The following Thursday he called again.

"Hey, what's up? This is Derrick."

"Um, yeah. What can I do for you Derrick?" I said, bracing myself for a last minute cancellation. I could not believe he was going to cancel at the last minute.

"Listen, I have to cancel your lesson. I have a gig tonight. We'll have to do it some other time."

"I see. Well, you know what Derrick? I don't think this is going to work out. Thanks Anyway," I said, and hung up. *No more tolerations.*

I asked Mary to find me another instructor. After making inquiries at various shops, Mary suggested Kirk. He had many years of experience and sounded nice on the phone.

When I went for the first lesson I was a bit apprehensive, thinking about Derrick and his unprofessionalism. Kirk led me to a room next to the store which was little more than a closet with a window. He seemed like a complete throw-back to the 80s, with long black hair and blunt cut bangs, but, he was very polite and had kind eyes and an engaging smile.

"Have a seat right here, darlin'" he said, pointing to one of two stools. He showed me how to properly hold the guitar, and insisted that the size of my still-small hands would not be a deterrent to playing. He seemed like a very happy person.

"So, how long have you been doing this?" I asked him.

"Honey, I've been playing guitar since before you were a glimmer in your father's eyes," he said, repositioning my hand on the guitar neck, "and I've been teaching for over twenty years."

I liked him. So, I purchased the instruction manual he suggested. Each week we would go over one new song in the book and learn a new chord. Kirk also requested that I choose a song that I would like to play. We worked on my first choice "Sweet Home Alabama" for several weeks before I requested a new song. It seemed like each song I picked, was too difficult for me, but I kept trying.

***

Journal Entry: 12-27-2011

I won a trip to Costa Rica!
At least, I think I did.
I received a letter in the mail that says I have won an all-expense paid trip to Costa Rica. I don't even remember entering a contest. I'm sure it's a scam. I called and left a message at the number listed, but they probably won't call back until after the holidays. It's probably a scam. I never win anything. But, what if it's not...

Chapter Thirteen
New Year's Eve

January

We finally found a parking spot, probably illegal, in front of a million dollar cottage a few streets from the beach. Piling out of the dark green minivan, we divvied up the supplies we would need for celebrating New Year's Eve. I lugged the beach chairs, my Dad had the cooler, and my Mom, my sister, and Dalton trailed behind.

The street was already filling with families, and all of them seemed to be heading toward the sand. We made our way down the boardwalk and onto the beach. I spotted my sister. My mother was huffing and puffing her way through the sand. I managed to spread our belongings out in a rectangle to mark off "our" territory so that no one would walk in front of us and block the fireworks.

The beach was already almost full at 6 p.m. The fireworks wouldn't start for hours, but my mom insisted on getting to the beach early, which necessitated coolers of food and drink, which we set up in the middle of our little area. My mom was a big fan of fireworks and would always clap and cheer throughout the entire fireworks display.

Sitting in my beach chair, I thought back to the prior year. Bryan had been with me for the fireworks. It occurred to me that for most family events I had a date. There was always some kind of buffer between my family and me. When I was married, I had Carlos. His presence meant that the conversation would never get too personal. Bryan brought an easy-going vibe to any situation. Everybody loved Bryan. Now, I had to negotiate these events on my own.

Dalton was fussing as usual, complaining about being bored. In order to pass the time, I suggested a game. It was a variation of a game we had played once or twice at family events. My Dad, who usually hated games and generally refused to play them throughout my childhood, had invented it. Someone would write the names of famous people throughout history on little pieces of paper, and then tape one to each person's forehead. That way everyone could see each other's character, except the person wearing the name. We would go around the circle asking "yes or no" questions about who we were.

This time we didn't have paper or tape, so I had to change it to just "Guess Who I'm Thinking Of." It took a little while to get going, but soon everyone was taking turns, guessing and giving clues. "I'm thinking of a famous politician," I started.

"Are you dead or alive?" my Dad asked.

"I'm dead," I replied.

"Roosevelt," my Mom chimed in.

"Nope," I said.

"Obama!" Dalton said, settling into the sand next to me.

97

"Nope" I smiled.

"Was he one of the founding fathers?" my Dad asked.

"Nope"

"Kennedy!" my Mom declared.

"Yep."

"I knew it!" she exclaimed. After that, there was lots of guessing and joking and the time passed quickly. Famous, dead singers seemed to be the most popular choice for famous people. In no time, the fireworks were beginning. I tried to capture them with the camera on my phone, but none of the pictures came out very good and suddenly they were over.

I always hated this part. After the fireworks ended, it would take forever for the traffic to clear. To pass the time, we played the guessing game again, and an easy camaraderie filled the car. Before we knew it, we were able to make it out onto the main road.

Instead of driving directly home, we decided to drive through Victoria Park, a neighborhood in which the houses were always decorated elaborately with Christmas lights. Entering the neighborhood, we were happy to see that the Christmas decorations were still up, even thought it was New Year's Eve. The glowing, colored lights always made me happy, and of course my mom cheered from the front seat.

House after house was decorated with all sorts of lights, each one seemingly trying to outdo the next. There were nativity scenes on some lawns and on others, inflatable Disney characters. Grae and I were in the back seat, reminding me of our younger days. It felt strange to be riding in the backseat again together, a real flashback to childhood.

We opened the side doors to better see the Christmas lights. Dad maneuvered the van through the traffic, and I took pictures, as our little group made its way through the neighborhood. Oddly enough, everything felt okay.

Chapter Fourteen
Fleeting

Journal Entry 1-7-2012

Mary found someone to rent my guest room again, finally. The extra money will really help, and Teresa seems really cool.

Now that I'm in the middle of the experiment, I don't know how I feel about it. I guess I thought it would be kind of a linear change, as if life would get better and better and my interest in men would diminish inversely. But I get these mad crushes, which last for a day or so and then disappear.

***

I was at my former employer's building, and my office suddenly felt way too small. The man across from me was saying something about a grant we were working on, but I just kept staring at the way his hair was cut, buzzed up the sides and short on top. He had been hired recently, and had come to me weeks ago to discuss something. We had ended up talking about the problems he had adjusting to his new position. I gave him advice both on navigating the office politics and on the importance of clearing up ambiguities early on.

After that, he kept coming to my office. And it really didn't help that he was a nice looking guy, obviously smart, with a good character. His lips were moving, but I couldn't quite focus on what he was saying... *I wonder what it would be like to spend time with him outside of work. He was probably very interesting to talk to...*

And here I was in the middle of a year-long experiment on *not dating*... I could feel the heat rise up from my collar and slowly ascend my neck. His predecessor had been my subordinate, so it made sense that he would pop by occasionally. But, now I was a contractor. There was no reason for this guy to keep stopping by. He seemed to be looking for excuses to come by.

He was saying something about a grant and the timeline, but, I was noticing the shape of his lips... *Really, what is wrong with me?* My palms were sweaty. I shifted in my seat, and I leaned across the desk on my elbows. My chest tightened. I couldn't breathe. This meeting had to end.

"Okay, so that sounds good," I said, rising from my chair. He looked up, startled. I went over and opened the door wider, in an obvious suggestion that he pass through it. "Yes, let's talk again soon," I said, feeling the heat reach my cheeks in a flush. *How am I going to make it through a year?*

After that, I tried to focus on his flaws. For one thing, he was entirely too young for me. He looked like he was in his late twenties, thirty at most. By my estimation, that made him at least fifteen years too young for me. *Soooo, not interested. Period. End of Story.* And, yet, he kept coming to mind. *Damn, I hate crushes. They are so illogical. They come on strong and you only see what you want to see. Like this guy, what is he hiding?*

Chapter Fifteen
Jamie on Art

I was standing in front of a big, rectangular canvas propped against a tall, metal easel. Jamie was on the other side of the classroom, washing some brushes in the sink. Even though we were alone, I felt comfortable with him. He was very low-key, the kind of guy who probably got kicked around quite a bit in the past, and as a result became somewhat sensitive. He seemed comfortable in the quiet, campus-like arts center in the heart of Bonita Springs. Maybe he could just blend in and disappear, doing his art and coordinating the classes from behind the scenes.

Today, he was teaching the drop-in art class, which consisted of me and me alone. No one else ever showed up, but, I didn't mind. I got all the instruction to myself.

"Jamie," I said looking at the painting in front of me. The painting of a pair of thigh-high boots was progressing rather slowly. "How come some people seem to have a drive to create, while others do not? I find it very difficult to make myself sit down and do it." He looked up from the brushes.

"Well, I think it's different for everybody. It's kind of like working out. Sometimes you have to force yourself to go to the gym, but once you do, you feel good." I looked out one of the windows with the evening sun shining through. "I want to be one of those people who can spend hours alone, doing whatever…" I said wistfully. He didn't reply.

At home, I had to force myself to work on the paintings, but I was always glad when I did. I felt like I was impersonating "a real artist" when I set up the easel and paints. I would place the computer to the left of the canvas on my desk and search for a photo I liked, choosing music to inspire the process, mostly random songs from Pandora. Today, I couldn't seem to find an image that really motivated me.

When I was in high school, I had experimented with different media, like painting and drawing. I think I liked the mysterious air of the artist. I took an army medical jacket and covered it in paint splatters and cut the fingers off a brown leather glove and attached a large jewel to it. My friend Lisa and I experimented with elaborate eye make-up, applying it with a tiny brush to make fantastical designs around our eyes. At that point in our lives, we didn't care what anyone else thought. As a matter of fact, I think we were daring people to say something.

My family moved just before my senior year of high school. I had no real plan for the future, but my new art teacher encouraged me to apply to art school. I felt proud of the pieces I was creating, so I went ahead and applied to the Museum School of Art in Boston. My father went with me to the interview, which was intimidating but exhilarating. I wondered what it would be like to focus solely on learning to paint. I imagined working on huge canvases and learning all kinds of techniques in the company of really cool people.

But, when the time came time to talk about finances, I couldn't imagine how to pay the tuition or figure out how to pay for an apartment in Boston. My dad said we could figure it out somehow, but I knew it would never work. My parents had enough problems covering their own bills without dealing with mine. As we drove away, I pretty much crossed it off the list as a possibility for my future.

I was pleased when I was accepted to the Museum School, and shocked when it was announced at graduation, that I had been offered a $1,000 scholarship. But, I knew I had to take another direction. $1,000 would cover only a tenth of the tuition and I didn't feel strongly enough about an art career to put the energy into making it happen.

***

Journal Entry: 1-15-2011

I have been working on listening to myself all the time, or as often as possible, in terms of what I need. Sometimes, I just want to slow down, stop everything, and just relax or sleep. Sometimes I need to relax and don't know how. Yesterday, I had no energy. I was totally drained, but felt this anxious energy running through my body - as if it was stuck in my muscles.

I went to the gym and afterward I felt better. It's so hard to stay in sync with my actual needs. When I do, I feel stronger, and I have so much more to give. I think that by honoring your self by listening to it and acting on its needs, you increase your self-esteem.

Apparently, I'm going to Costa Rica. I guess the contest wasn't a scam. I leave it two weeks.

Chapter Sixteen
Roommate

Are you serious? The click of the front door had woken me up, again. This was the second day in a row that my renter woke me up at 5 a.m. I was livid. *Why the heck does she have to work out at 5 a.m.?! What a freak!* I tried to get back to sleep, but ended up, tossing and turning for an hour.

I managed to get in another half hour of sleep, before getting up at 7:00 a.m. to get ready for work. Today was the weekly management meeting at 9:00 a.m. I couldn't concentrate on what was being said and when it was my turn I barely managed to make a coherent presentation.

"...And so...yes, the report is due in one week... um... I'll need Kathy's input by Wednesday... Um...... that's all."

I didn't see my new renter, Teresa, again until the following evening when she came in the front door, talking on her cell phone. She had only been there for two weeks but I was starting to wonder if it would work out. She walked right into her side of the apartment, completely oblivious. She entered the kitchen a little while later wearing a robe, her long, curly hair up in a towel, still talking on the phone.

She always ate dinner for breakfast and breakfast for dinner, which struck me as odd. *Who am I to judge? My eating habits are strange enough.* As she began preparing her meal, I said "Hey, you woke me up at 5 a.m. again."

"Oh, I'm sorry. I tried to close the door softly. Isn't the machine working?" She pointed at the sound machine I had placed next to the front door. "Yes, but it's the click of the lock mechanism, not the door that wakes me up."

"Not sure what to do about that," she said offhandedly.

Oh my God, I want to strangle her, I thought. In the past I would have gone over to Bryan's, complained, and gotten it out of my system. Now, I could only stew on it. Later that day, I called the handyman to work on the lock. He wouldn't be able to come by for two more days. That night, I put a pillow over my ears and turned the sound machine up. I slept better just knowing the handyman was on his way.

I paid him $40 to file down the edge of the door and realign the locking mechanism, but at 4:45 a.m. the next morning there was still a click. *That's it, I have had it!* That evening, when she was in the kitchen I said "Listen, you woke me up at 4:45 am again. This isn't working."

"Well, I don't know what to tell you. I close the door as quietly as I can. I'm not sure what more I can do."

Okay, no more tolerations, I thought remembering what I had rehearsed in my head. "You have two choices. You can either change your morning routine or find another place to live."

She looked surprised. "I told you before I moved in that I go to the gym in the morning," she said smugly.

"Yes, and I told you that that was fine as long as you didn't wake me up... and you are. I'm not going to argue with you," I said, and walked away.

The next day, she told me she was going to move, but would need until the end of the month. Three whole weeks. I wanted her out immediately, but agreed. A week later she complained that all of the places she was interested in had application processes and wouldn't be ready until the following month. I told her "That's not my problem. The locks are going to be changed on March 1st." Somehow, she found a place that she could move into by the first.

***

Journal Entry: 1-28-2012 Adoption

Today when I was out I noticed a family with an adopted girl and I realized that my feelings about adoption are changing. I am enjoying my life so much now that I no longer feel a strong desire for children. What was I trying to do with adopting? Solve my own childhood issues? Was I trying to take care of the child inside of me? My inner child feels 100% cared for now compared to how I felt four months ago. My need for fun and play is fulfilled. I feel cared for, protected and listened to. Maybe I was looking for a man to take care of me. Now that I can do all that for myself, I don't feel the need for a man, and I don't feel the need to take care of a child. I do feel like spending time with my nieces and nephews, but just for the fun of it.

Chapter Seventeen
Jeanie & Consulting

Jeffrey is the chief fundraising expert on my team. We were sitting on a bench together on Happehatchee's porch, across from Jeanie. She had invited us to come and counsel her on starting a fundraising program. "I don't have a background in nonprofit management," she had said, "so any advice would be really valuable to me." I was glad she was interested in "growing" Happehatchee, but I was concerned that the board might not be ready to fund the growth. "If I can't get the board to pay for it, I'll pay for it out of my own pocket." she had said.

Happehatchee had virtually no fundraising infrastructure, so as we sat together on the porch Jeffrey explained to Jeanie the theory and practice of fundraising. He seemed quite at home in his seersucker suit and tie, despite the fact that he was born and bred in the North. I loved Jeffrey. He was one of my favorite people, a genuinely good person with an irreverent sense of humor. If he didn't prefer men I definitely would have been interested in him.

"The most important thing is the database," he told Jeanie. "You have to centralize your efforts around the database." Volunteers and visitors kept coming and going and Jeanie excused herself several times to deal with issues that arose. I wondered whether she would be able to implement the things we were discussing. I wasn't sure whether she had enough support to make any changes. *This place is a disaster,* I thought. *It would take a miracle to turn it around.*

Afterwards, Jeffrey and I talked about how much of a cultural change it would take to get anything accomplished at Happehatchee. A few days later, Jeanie met me at the gate in front of my condo with cash to pay for the consulting session. I felt bad that she couldn't get the board to approve the expense and was paying for it herself. I had never had a client pay for consulting with their own cash, but I had to remind myself that my time and expertise were valuable and that I had to pay Jeffrey.

***

Journal Entry: 2-11-2012

This week was stressful and I didn't get to do anything fun or creative. I'm also a bit stressed about leaving for my upcoming trip with that woman here. She keeps waking me up at ungodly hours of the morning. Looking forward to having my own place again...to coming home and being in my own space. Luckily, Carlos said he would stay here while I'm gone. That freaked her out!

Chapter Eighteen
Another World

February

Bright blue bags hung amongst the wide green leaves above our heads. Each bag encased a stalk full of Costa Rican bananas. The bananas were surrounded by the blue, plastic cocoons to protect them from insects and weather fluctuations. Our guide, one of the professors from Earth University, was explaining the use of an onion-based pesticide, equally as effective as the chemical pesticides currently in use by many banana plantations.

The "Be an Earth Student for a Week" trip had finally begun. After searching my memory, I had remembered entering a contest on the Whole Foods Web Site. Apparently, my entry was chosen over more than 500,000 entries. Our little group consisted of me, the other two contest winners, two representatives from Whole Foods and three organic food bloggers. We were eight strangers, thrust together for a week. We had met up in San Jose and boarded a little, white bus that would be the only constant on this amazing trip.

The bus brought us to the middle of a banana plantation miles from civilization. We stood around, shifting from one foot to another in the soft ground, listening to the technical aspects of sustainable agriculture, dwarfed by the wide banana trees surrounding us. The rows that seemed to stretch for miles. I snapped photos of the verdant green all around me, delighting in the endless shapes and patterns. I noticed some of my teammates had quizzical looks on their faces. Clearly, they were not seeing what I was seeing.

I thought about the interesting diversity of the group. Aisha was originally from Pakistan, and had won the trip. She was a thin girl in her mid-twenties with coffee colored skin and dark, dark eyes. She wore a wide-brimmed, navy-colored canvas hat for protection from the sun. April, a blogger from LA, was a tiny girl with a pixie haircut and an infectious smile. She was studiously taking notes in a little notebook.

Max, owner of livingmaxwell.com, was videotaping the conversation from behind a camera mounted on a tall tripod. He was a good looking guy, he was in his early thirties with coal black eyes that contrasted his prematurely-graying hair. Max was from New York City and seemed very cool and sophisticated. Like most people on the trip, he chatted mostly about what we were seeing and not too much about himself.

"Earth University sells bananas to support the university and to provide hands-on instruction for the students," the professor told us. "This banana field is a living laboratory." Jose and Marta, a Hispanic couple from Texas, seemed bored. Jose was shifting back and forth on his hips, and Marta was staring off into space. Although Jose grew up in the States, and had perfect English, Marta was from Mexico and while her English was a little shaky, she seemed like a very sweet person.

"The University uses sustainable banana production, in which the various parts of the banana operation are separated to minimize stress to the land," the professor continued. "The packing plant is located far from the banana fields, as opposed to the very centralized, traditional banana production. Let's head over to the packing plant now," he said, turning back toward the van.

"Sustainable agriculture is actually less efficient, but far better for the land. Students come from all over Latin America to learn about it," he said, as we walked. "They then bring the knowledge and practices they learn back to their home countries where they implement changes." *I wonder if there is any data to prove the changes they are making in the world. If they could prove their impact, they would have a strong case for support from donors.*

When we arrived at the packing house, I was reminded once again how lucky I am not to work in a factory. The bananas come in on a suspended conveyor line directly from the jungle, after which they are rinsed with a high pressure water gun. April hammed it up for the camera by spraying some hanging bananas. "Next, the bananas are deposited in these vats for further rinsing," the professor said as we followed him through the plant. Workers, who were all from the local area, were busy at various stages of the process. They had scarves covering their heads, long gloves, and waterproof aprons.

At least the building has no walls, I thought. *Kind of like working outside. That must make it a little more pleasant.* We moved along to where the banana bunches were cut, dried, and stamped before being placed in boxes and ultimately shipped out. One woman's sole job was to place stickers on banana bunches as they went by. I thought back to the many blue-collar jobs I had when I was starting out. I had gone from cleaning hotel rooms to waitressing, to bar tending, to cutting hair, until I finally broke into the white-collar world of management. I had tried to enjoy every step along the way, but I had no envy for the women working here in the stifling heat and humidity.

On the way back to the university, we talked about our plans. Liz, a young executive from Whole Foods seemed to be enjoying the trip as much as the winners. She was thin and cool-looking in her aviator sunglasses and cap. "Earth University sits on 8,342 acres in the heart of Costa Rica," she explained. "We will be spending three days there, both in classrooms and out in the fields. Then, we will head to the coast for a few days of R&R before flying back," she said, smiling.

"Everyone has a private room at the university, which will allow us all to sleep soundly and to get up early. You'll need to be at breakfast by 6:00 a.m. and on the bus by 6:30," Liz said. *Okay, what?! I am soooo not a morning person,* I thought with alarm. I wondered how that would work out.

On the way to dinner, I got a chance to talk with Aisha and April. We were all sitting together at the back of the bus. They were both students. Aisha was finishing an MA in psychology, and April was working on her bachelor's degree. I told them about my current business and that the trip was inspiring me to work internationally.

"Hey, my roommate does program evaluation too. She works all over the world. I could hook you up with her if you like," Aisha said.

"Wow! That would be awesome. I would love to pick her brain."

At dinner that night, I sat next to Max, who told me about how he started his blog.

"After graduating from college, I moved to New York City in order to work in finance. The high-pressure job led to some fast living, too many late nights and some self-destructive behavior," he said. "I realized that I needed to live differently, so I committed to making some serious changes. I quit drinking alcohol in 1999. I quit smoking cigarettes in 2000, and in 2001 I stopped taking antidepressants after nearly eleven years. I've never relapsed once on any of it."

"Wow Max, that's really quite amazing." I said. He kept looking down the table at Liz and I smiled. *Men.*

"As health became a priority for me, I started to educate myself about conventional food. It shocked me that nearly everything we eat is tainted with toxic pesticides, insecticides... growth hormones... or artificial preservatives. I wanted to treat my body with the most nutritious and 'clean' food possible, so I switched to organic." Max looked over at Liz. My ego was bruised a bit that he would be looking at her while talking to me. *Yes, he's definitely evolved, but still a guy.*

"Not only did it give me more energy, but it helped to change my relationship with food. I started to view food as medicine. I wanted to share that knowledge, so I started my blog. If it weren't for the blog, I wouldn't be sitting here," he said. I appreciated his enthusiasm, but I thought it was funny that he would be interested in a girl who was half his age.

I felt like I was watching the whole scene from a distance. He had literally no interest in me or my life, only in himself. In the past I would have overlooked his wandering eye and been caught up in his story, losing myself in the fairy tale I was creating in my head and calculating how he would fit into my "perfect life" scenario.

How many times have I overlooked that kind of behavior with men? I thought. I would get so caught up in my own fantasy of who I wanted them to be, that I would ignore the obvious truth: that were completely self-centered and totally uninterested. *Note to self: self-centeredness is quite unattractive...*

We arrived home quite late that night, but I was indeed up by 6 and on the bus by 6:30 the next morning. The bus was unusually quiet. Everyone seemed to be struggling to wake up. We were headed to a tour of an experimental field lab. We arrived, and it felt like we were stepping into a vivid quilt of colors. Brilliant green plants contrasted with the garnet-colored shrubs and the rich brown soil. Our little group crowded around the instructor, Alex Pacheco Bustos, who was wearing a wide-brimmed hat, woven out of navy and cream-colored cords.

"It is here that our professors and students come up with ingenious solutions to agricultural challenges," he explained in Spanish. One of the students translated into English. "In many countries there is poor soil quality and limited acreage. We work to help farmers all over the world to overcome these challenges."

Some of their designs included using recycled items, like plastic bottles and pieces of tires mixed into the soil to extend the amount. They also added coconut shells, an abundant resource in Latin America, to the soil to both extend it and to provide "substrate," for the plants to grow on.

We broke into teams to learn in a more "hand's-on" fashion about vertical agriculture. I looked around, and

116

everybody had already teamed up. *Great, I'll have to build it by myself,* I thought. It felt just like gym class growing up. I had moved so often that I never seemed to have friends when critical moments like choosing partners for gym class came up.

I got some materials, and started mixing coconut shells and soil. I shoveled some of the coconut shell substrate into a thick plastic tube, which was tied at the ends. The instructor came over and said, "Muy bien!" He took out a knife and made slits in a spiral design up the sides of the tube. The seedlings were placed in the holes. Voila! A Vertical Planter. We hung up all of the planters, which ended up looking like a row of thick, silver sausages. It felt good to know that little plants would be growing in them soon.

Later we had a soil class in the laboratory, where I got to practice some of my long- forgotten chemistry. Standing around in lab coats, I remembered my interest in the subject and also my boredom with lab work. Everyone else seemed intimidated by chemistry and by the equipment. When the professor announced that he needed an assistant, no one stepped forward. "I'll do it," I said, walking forward and taking the lab coat. My trip-mates looked on appreciatively as I handled the equipment with relative ease, and asked and answered questions thoughtfully. I was truly fascinated with soil chemistry.

Another highlight was the trip to Macho Loco's farm. Our goal was to build a "bio-digester" for use on his farm. We each had a small part in building the system, which was designed to convert animal waste to a gas for use in cooking and heating their home. Our instructor Juan was a handsome, young professor who was in charge of outreach programs to the local community. He introduced us to Macho Loco, a big, strapping guy with a goatee and a bandana covering his long, curly hair. He looked more like a pirate than a farmer.

The house was made of concrete, and the small outbuildings were a combination of wood and tin. As we wandered through the farm, we passed by pigs, chickens, and ducks roaming around. There was a very long, wide, ditch already dug behind the pig sty. Juan instructed a few of the guys to unroll a gigantic, thick sea-foam green, plastic bag along the ditch. This is where the liquid waste would collect and turn into methane. We were each invited to play a small part in assembling the biodigester. My moment consisted of attaching a hose to something. I was actually more interested in looking around at that moment.

There was something special about Macho's farm. It wasn't incredibly advanced, perhaps just the opposite. It was sort of primitive. It looked like things were worked on as needed, projects sometimes dropped or forgotten. Maybe it was the lighting. Although not hot, the sunlight illuminated everything brightly. Things seemed to be sprouting up and growing everywhere, and Macho took pride in pointing out his accomplishments.

Maybe it was the sense of peace that blanketed the property. Time seemed to stand still. Macho's wife came by with a child on her hip and a little girl trailing her. I realized that Macho was a king. *He lives in perfect harmony with this land, planting when he needs to and resting when it's time to rest, living totally in the moment.* I felt a tremendous surge of envy. I wanted that kind of feeling in my life.

Undoubtedly, one of the biggest highlights of the trip was when I gave the valedictory speech on our final night. Somehow, I had been elected the day before to give the speech. Alyce, a blogger for the Motley Fool, had come up to me as we were waiting for the bus and said "I guess they need someone to give a short speech about our experiences on the trip. Max and I thought you might like to do it."

"Well, sure," I said, I guess so." I wondered what I was getting myself into. Later that day, I went around and interviewed each of my trip-mates about their experiences. I really wondered why they picked me. Was it because I was the most articulate? The most thoughtful? Perhaps the most likely to be willing to stand up and give a speech in public. I didn't care. *I won. They picked me. Screw gym class.*

It seemed that each person had taken something different away from the experience. April wanted me to include something about the workers. Aisha felt a real connection to her place in the consumption process and her power as a consumer. When I asked Max what the trip meant to him, he said "Well, really, for me it has restored my faith."

The University provided graduation caps and gowns and we nervously dressed backstage. Luckily, not many people would be attending the event so the room was mostly empty. I peeked out from behind the curtain. Dr. Jose Zaglul president of the university, was sitting with the Whole Foods executives at a table to the right of the podium.

Although I can, and often do, speak in public, I get nervous every time. As I stepped up to the podium and looked out over the audience, I tried to calm my racing heart. *Focus,* I thought. I had never given a speech in Spanish before, and as I glanced at the notes I'd written in English, it occurred to me what a brazen choice I'd made, to deliver the speech in Spanish. *I'll have to translate my notes as I go, Geez!* I could feel hives forming on my neck.

My speech was called "Semillas de Inspiracion" or "Seeds of Inspiration."

"Good evening," I said in Spanish. "My group asked me to convey to you the sentiments of our trip. I would like to do so in Spanish. Please forgive any mistakes I may make." I looked at the president and he smiled.

"We have experienced so many things over the last few days. It is difficult to express our gratitude and respect for all that you accomplish here at Earth University. From our time out in the banana fields up until today, we have felt the love that you put into everything that you do. The effects of this trip will stay with us for a lifetime. Some of the effects we are not even aware of yet.

"One of the most important things that we have come to understand is the part that we play as consumers. We are beginning to understand the influence that we have, and we have developed a connection to concepts that were previously abstract. We see now how things are grown, and we see our part in the process.

"We have worked beside the workers, and felt your respect for them at all levels of production." I looked over and found April's face. "Some of us are looking forward to learning more about the protection of the workers in the banana industry in Latin America.

"We deeply appreciate the way that you are touching the community in different ways and attacking poverty. One of the things that has touched us profoundly is the concept that the world must invest in sustainability if it is to survive. We can no longer think only of the present;

we must think of our future as well and invest in sustainable practices.

"As for myself, this trip has touched me both professionally and personally." I braced myself to say what I felt I had to. "As a professional who evaluates the effectiveness of organizations for a living, I am always looking at impact. I want to know not only what an organization is doing, but what changes they are making in the community.

"Both I and your donors want to know what your students are doing and accomplishing once they go back to their home countries. Give us the statistics and numbers we need to understand how the world is changing as a result of your efforts. How many new agricultural businesses have been started in Latin America by former students? How many students are currently employed by multinationals worldwide?

"On a personal level, if I had a goal for this trip it was to rejuvenate myself. And although I have seen and heard and learned much, have gotten up early and stayed up late, my body is tired, but my soul is satisfied. For me, as an artist, seeing all the vivid colors and sounds of Costa Rica has touched me deeply. As a human being, the connections to all of the people on this trip is what has affected me. The love and the openness of the staff and the students is what I will take with me."

Some of my team mates had tears in their eyes.

"The peace that I felt on Macho Loco's farm, I will take with me. But most importantly, many of us work alone in this fight to change the world. Being here and learning from you has restored our faith, in sustainability, and in the future. And that... we will take with us. Thank you."

The entire room was clapping. As I descended from the platform, my tripmates came up and congratulated me on the speech. Over dinner I chatted with Dr. Zaglul, who seemed impressed with the part about measuring impact, and my trip-mates and I reminisced about our experiences at the University. Everyone seemed a little sad about leaving, but also excited to have a chance to spend some time at the beach.

Liz surprised us the next day, announcing "We thought that since you've travelled all this way, you might like to experience a real rainforest, so we will be making a brief stop on the way to the beach." *That sounds cool. What a great bonus and it'll break the long bus ride up nicely.*

On the way, the lowlands gradually turned into highlands, and the trees became denser. When we arrived at our destination, we all piled into a tram that would take us to the bottom. The tram had two separate cars which carried us through the canopy of trees. I looked back and saw Kate looking out serenely as we floated past lush, green vegetation on our way to the bottom.

We disembarked and as I walked along, I was enveloped by the majesty of the rain forest. Our guide described the plants and insects, and I felt like I was absorbing all the green around me. I stopped for a photo under the biggest tree I had ever seen. Our little group continued in single file along the path. The grandeur and quiet dignity of the rainforest affected all of us as we marched along.

Back at the visitor's station, we gathered on the platform.

"Hey, would anyone like to go zip lining?" Kate asked. "We have plenty of time," I looked around at the enthusiastic faces. *Seriously? I'm the only one who doesn't want to go zip lining?* I had gone zip lining years ago with a friend, and had been glad to try it in New Hampshire as part of a ropes course, but I didn't see any allure at the thought of speeding along over the tops of already high trees in a foreign country. *I have nothing to prove.*

"I'll catch up with all of you later," I said, and headed off for the gift shop, where, I spent twenty minutes picking out the perfect cutting board. I decided on one made of alternating shades of hard wood and I bought a similar one for my mom. It wasn't until later, when I was showing it to Aisha on the bus, that I realized I had helped contribute to the destruction of the rainforest in purchasing that cutting board. *Well, there's no going back. I better cut up a lot of vegetables with this thing.*

It was quite late when we arrived at the hotel in Manzanillo. It didn't feel very much like a hotel. It was a little village of bungalows, each connected with a boardwalk. Each of my tripmates had a private A-frame bungalow. This was definitely the Beverly Hills version of "roughing it." Each bungalow had a thatched roof, crisp white linens, hard wood floors, two double beds and a Jacuzzi.

The next day, some of us headed to the beach, while the others took the van into town. I asked Kate if she wanted to do yoga on the beach. It was the first time we'd had a chance to chat alone, and I was curious as to what her life was like. We were about the same age, and she had a very high-profile job with Whole Foods as their director of public relations. As we lay on our towels in the white sand, I realized that one thing we had in common was our exhaustion. *Women of my generation clearly work too much, I thought.*

I had promised to lead the yoga flow, and eventually we got up and moved our towels closer to the shoreline, where the sand was firmer. I began going through the yoga sequence I had developed for myself, and it dawned on me that I was not an actual yoga teacher. For some reason, I always have the idea that I can do anything until I am actually in the moment doing it. "Uh, and then you kind of sweep your arm over your head like this...Yes, that's it," I said, as a light mist from the breaking waves fell over us. *Okay, what's next?* I thought. Kate was a very forgiving yoga student, but eventually we gave up and just hung out on the beach.

On the last day, after we had all spent a bit of time dolphin-watching and shopping in town, I climbed into a big blue, hammock I found at the beach. Palm trees shaded the area, and decided to write in my journal. But with the sound of the waves crashing on the beach, the soft breeze blowing through the palm fronds above and the hammock gently rocking me, I soon fell into a long, deep sleep.

That night at dinner we all shared contact information, promising to keep in touch. Back home, we all connected on Facebook, and managed to maintain contact in greater and lesser degrees. It is always fun to see updates on how my tripmates lives are progressing.

***

Journal Entry: 2-25-2012

It's our last day in Manzanillo. We leave in an hour. I'm just waiting for the jacuzzi to fill so I can enjoy this one last bit of luxury before I leave. The trip has been amazing, and, what I have found most interesting has been how I've felt interacting with my tripmates. With some of them I have felt more comfortable than with others. But in all cases I have felt a bit off-center. We've had so many incredible experiences, one right after another, but there has been little time to be alone, in order to feel centered. In the past, I haven't spent as much time alone, but now see that I need it.

I have been thinking about how to change my life. I don't think I can put up with it the way it was. I don't want to deal with the amount of stress I have been putting up with. It's not the life for me. I want to keep the parts of my life that I like and transform the rest. I would rather fix it than change it completely. This trip is bringing back my desire to work internationally but I wouldn't want to move to another county. Maybe I can just consult internationally. I would need to have a more flexible lifestyle to make that possible. I feel like getting rid of the condo. I need to figure out just how much of a home base I really need.

Chapter Nineteen
Girls Day

I wanted to strengthen my family ties in order to reduce my reliance on men, so I talked to my cousin Gabrielle about having a Girls' Day with my mother and my sisters. On a Saturday, Gabrielle and I picked up my mother and then headed out to meet my sisters downtown.

We were on our way to Fifth Avenue, the trendy, upscale part of town. I had a rough idea of what we would do, but on the way the agenda changed several times as mom thought of different ways to spend the day. Since Gabrielle lived two hours north of Naples, I thought Fifth Avenue would be a good starting point for a tourist.

"Oh, look! There's an art show. Let's stop there," my mother exclaimed.

"Mom, Garan just texted me saying she's hungry," I replied. *When did this become a democracy?* I thought. I organized this day, b*ut I should be open to other people's opinions and ideas...*

"Well, what about the Venetian Village?" she asked. I looked over at my cousin and wondered if she would like the Venetian Village. "Mom, Gabrielle came all the way from Punta Gorda to spend the day with us. I think we should go to Fifth Avenue. Besides, Garan is hungry and there's nowhere cheap to eat at Venetian Village."

"Fine," she said gruffly.

I felt sorry for my mother. She was always tired. At 68, she was still working part-time at a department store, and part-time helping my dad with his business. Any other free time was eaten up babysitting for my seven nieces and nephews. She hardly ever took time for herself, and probably really needed some fun. I wanted to accommodate her, but there were other needs to consider.

Fifth Avenue is the wealthy and fashionable part of Naples, where people go to see and be seen. It's a good place to take a tourist, but I never feel quite comfortable there. We were sitting at a little table in front of a café when Giselle joined us, looking chic and skinny. We had formed something of a truce. "Hi everybody," she said, barely looking at me. We all spent a little time catching up over lunch. None of us had seen Gabrielle in months, and there was quite a bit to talk about, especially with all the new babies in the family.

After lunch we walked up Fifth Avenue, admiring the beautiful clothes and gifts in the windows. Standing in front of a store, the conversation turned to where we would go next.

"I want to go to Venetian Village," my mother said.

"We want to get a drink," Giselle said, referring to her and Grae. I looked over at my cousin and tried to think of somewhere a tourist would like to go.

"Come on, we can walk around Venetian Village," my mother said.

They kept going around and around. My stomach tied itself into knots.

"Listen everybody; let's go to the Naples Beach Club. We can have a drink on the deck and Gabrielle can see the hotel," suggested Giselle. They continued to argue. *Why do women have this much trouble making a decision?* I thought. Everyone seemed to be advocating for their own position, without considering what was best for the group.

Finally, I said "Okay. Enough. We're going to the hotel," and we headed out.

My mother pouted, saying that I never listened to her, but she eventually agreed.

At the Naples Beach Club, we sat at a bar right on the beach and had the waiter take a picture of us. Everyone relaxed, and we talked about life in southwest Florida and about the past. Since we were close in age, Gabrielle and I had spent a lot of time together when we were growing up. She had lived in Connecticut, close to my grandparents. Although she was adopted, I never thought of her that way, maybe because she looked Italian to me, just like the rest of the family.

"It's so good to see you all. I wish we lived closer," Gabrielle said.

"What have you been up to lately, Gabrielle?" Giselle asked her, leaning back against the railing.

"Well, you know, I work for Habitat for Humanity now. As a matter of fact, I went to one of Geva's seminars a few months ago on fundraising. I'm really busy with that. I run the office for them and we've been building so many homes this year." Gabrielle looked tired.

"That's so cool," Garan said

"And my youngest daughter is graduating from high school this year," Gabrielle went on.

I thought about how different our lives were. She had had children young, had stayed married to the same man all these years and had entered the nonprofit world recently. I had married late, divorced relatively quickly, and been in the nonprofit world for almost a decade.

Time wore on, and my sisters started talking about getting food.

"I want to stay and watch the sunset," my mother said.

"But Mom, there is only a bar menu here. Everybody is ready for dinner."

"Why don't we leave after the sunset?" she asked.

"Because Gabrielle has a long drive home, and it's dinner time. It's time to go. Come on." She was grumbling again about me being pushy, but we all piled into our cars and met up back at my mother's place for phase two: "An Evening of Pampering."

After some sandwiches, I brought out a bunch of supplies for pampering, with the idea that we would all take turns pampering each other. I got out buckets of hot water to soak our feet in and some pedicure supplies, some little packets of creams for facials and some hair treatments.

I instructed my mother on how to apply a treatment to her hair, while I was giving Grae a pedicure. Somehow, they just didn't get the reciprocal concept and I ended up doing almost all of the services. *Why are they just sitting*

129

there? I wondered. Why don't they work on each other? Grae looked so tired. *She runs around after a toddler all day,* I thought. *This was probably the first time she had had a pedicure in a long time, if not ever.* I tried to massage some of the fatigue out of her sore foot muscles.

Luckily, Giselle was willing to paint Garan's toenails, or I would have ended up doing everything. As I washed Gabrielle's feet I thought about how much people seem to need these days, and how little they have to give. My sisters are all married with children and spend their days and nights, expending tremendous amounts of energy and focus on their children. There is very little left for themselves.

It suddenly dawned on me how much the experiment was changing me and changing my life. Not only did I have the space in my head to conceive of an event such as "Girls' Day," I had the space in my life to organize it and enough of an energy reserve to pamper others. I realized that I had already come a long way and it was only February.

***

Journal Entry 2-18-2012

Man, Carlos pisses me off. It turns out that he didn't even stay over at the condo as he promised. And we had talked about going to a big dance performance, but he never called like he said he would. What a jerk. I don't think I'm going to be friends with him anymore. There is no requirement that says one has to stay friends with an ex-husband. He doesn't have a good character, and he lies about everything. Screw him.

Chapter Twenty
Ground Hog Day

A few days later, I made popcorn and watched Groundhog Day again, for probably the 7th time. It's my all-time favorite movie, an underground cult classic. Very few people realize how deep and profound this movie actually is. Bill Murray plays a weather man who is reluctantly sent to Punxsutawney, Pennsylvania to cover a story about a weather forecasting "rat"(as he calls it) for the fourth year in a row. On awakening the following day, he discovers that it's Groundhog Day all over again, and again, and again. At first, he uses this to his advantage, then finally comes the realization that he is doomed to spend the rest of eternity in the same place, seeing the same people doing the same things, every day.

But, what he eventually learns is that it's not the similarity or difference of the events of each day that is important, it's what you do with those days. His gradually changes from a self-centered and cynical man to one who is happy, engaged with life and connected to the people around him.

In the beginning of the film, he is surly and detached. His life seems to have no meaning, and very little joy. When he discovers that he is reliving the same day over and over, he resists, trying to bargain his way out of it.

When nothing works, he becomes depressed and even tries to kill himself. It is only when he gives up and accepts his circumstances that he is able to actually enjoy himself, only to be returned to life the next morning.

A parallel plot line involves his love interest. Initially, he tries to become the type of man that the object of his affection would desire. He adopts all of the activities and interests that he thinks she would like, but eventually he starts figuring out what he actually enjoys.

In the end, he's much more "in the moment," more relaxed, and happy. *I wonder if that is what will happen to me,* I thought. Maybe I was unconsciously playing out the theme of the movie in real life. I kept a journal of the experiment from day one. If the experiment was successful, maybe it could help other people to find happiness. Maybe the journal could be turned into a book. Maybe other people would see the value of taking time off from dating and relationships to focus on their own lives.

Well, if I'm going to write a book, I'll probably need a ghostwriter, because I really don't have time to write an actual book. Plus I'm too close to the subject matter. Could I really write a book? I thought. *Why not? I've done crazier things...Yes, I should probably find a ghostwriter, but where to begin? Perhaps, I could get Mary to help me find one.*

***

Journal Entry: 3-2-2012

I took the leap and asked my folks how they felt about me using their house as a home base so that I can consult internationally. Surprisingly, they said it would be fine, especially if I used the studio, and provided them with

132

a letter for the bank, saying that I was renting it, thereby helping to prevent a foreclosure. Somehow, I had forgotten that they were facing a possible foreclosure. Small detail. As soon as I heard that, my head started spinning and has been spinning ever since.

Journal Entry 3-4-2012

The kayaking meetup was cancelled today. I had really been looking forward to it. Most of the day was lonely. At one point I thought, "what if I am creating a very lonely lifestyle? What if international consulting a super lonely lifestyle? It's times like these when I think the experiment must be a failure. Maybe I should try harder to create a community of like-minded folks... Maybe I should work on cultivating the relationships I already have... Maybe I should take an inventory and figure out which relationships I should invest time in. I wonder if people get into dating simply because they feel lonely.

Chapter Twenty-one
A Visit

March

Maria is coming to visit! I hadn't seen Maria in ages. I got up early to start working on the special lunch I had in mind. When she and her husband Bill arrived it felt a little awkward. I had wondered why Maria had responded to my invitation to lunch with "Sure, *we'd* love to come." I hadn't invited both of them, but I liked Maria and wanted to spend time with her. *If I had a boyfriend this wouldn't be an issue,* I thought. I liked Bill. He reminded me of a cattle farmer for some reason, kind of a refined cowboy.

Lunch was pleasant. Bill shared stories from his days spent teaching high school science, and we chatted about the times when Maria and I had worked for the same foundation. I was hired by the foundation to manage two programs over the summer and to complete an evaluation of them. Both programs were a mess. Each had a laundry list of problems, some were structural and others bordered on illegal.

The programs were run by a board member who was travelling for the summer. Having a board member running programs seemed like a huge conflict of interest. If fact, everyone in and around the program had seemed to be related in some way. The size of the facility was too small to accommodate the number of people they were trying to serve. The staff had been hired as consultants, rather than as employees, which had tax implications. There were also some improper usages of funds. The problems went on and on.

I felt like the foundation should step away from the programs immediately, before its name was tarnished by a possible scandal. At the end of the summer, my recommendations included closing both programs. One, a truancy program, had some redeeming value. I suggested that if they wanted to keep it, a complete overhaul would be necessary.

The truancy program had consisted of five white, middle-aged, female "judges," as they called themselves. The judges would make the mostly Hispanic families with truant children come in and stand before them and answer as to why their son or daughter had been truant. Not only was the bloated program ineffective, I found the whole concept repulsive and degrading.

The board accepted my recommendations. They decided to close the main program and asked me to revise the truancy program, which is where Maria came in. When I heard her story I knew that she would be perfect. She had worked her way up from copywriter to newscaster in her native Ecuador. She was smart, she had great public relations skills, and she was looking for work. She was hired to assist me in revising the program, and then to become the coordinator. First we had to navigate the sea of political cronyism.

"I don't know how we made it through that mess," I said at lunch.

"Yes, it was unbelievable," Maria replied. "Those women were like sharks in a tank."

"You were amazing, how you handled them," I said "You stood right up to them and always with a smile."

Thinking back, I realized that everyone seemed to have a stake in the program. The list of people on the payroll included the registrar, two women who worked in the office, and the school psychologist. I started by firing the entire staff. I revised the framework of the program from being punitive to a counseling model. Maria had quite a bit of difficulty getting cooperation from the school district. Even the principal was resistant to the new approach, but eventually, the counseling model was put in place.

"We did it, didn't we?" Maria said, looking up from her salad.

"We sure did," I replied. It was in that moment that I realized that Maria was the kind of friend I wanted in my life, someone smart, brave and polished, with a great heart. She was loyal to the end. *Yes, I definitely want more people like Maria in my new life.*

After we finished our meal, we discussed what to do next. Of the three options I offered, Maria and Bill chose to visit the Koreshan State Park. At the park, we walked through nature trails, marveling at the beauty along the Estero River. The sun shone through the palms and lush foliage, intermittently baking the sandy trails and sending up a multitude of fragrances from the foliage.

I enjoyed sharing such a special place with them. Joy was in the air as we walked along, taking in the beauty all around us. But soon, it became apparent that we would need to slow down to accommodate Bill's bad leg. Maria or

I would stop to admire a plant or area, to give him time to catch up. They both seemed thrilled to spend time in the forest after living in an urban area for so long. Eventually, we needed to turn around in order to manage the length of the walk back. After saying our goodbyes we promised to get together again soon.

***

Journal Entry: 3-10-2012

I've been thinking a lot about how much fear and self-loathing women have because of the narrow roles that society trains us for. It's all about having a partner. If we don't have one, we are nothing. If we don't look a certain way, we are worthless and we hate ourselves.

Because we are constantly trying to be something false, we don't know who we truly are. If we don't know who we truly are, we are nothing. We are confused and hate our empty selves. I think it's only by experimenting and trying to figure out what we genuinely like and believe that we can figure out who we really "are." The real challenge is then to live in accordance with that. We have to consistently do what brings us joy and pleasure if we are to affirm our own value.

It's not as if I don't believe in love, but I feel like I don't need it anymore. Love is like crack cocaine. It gives you this crazy high and then you feel like nothing else matters unless you keep getting it. Why does our society feed this addiction? We are so sick.

Chapter Twenty-two
Delicious

As I walked through the courtyard, a gentle breeze was blowing. Flowers and vegetables were artfully arranged for sale on shelves to my right. Large umbrellas covered the tables on my left and raucous conversation filled the air. The patrons were a mix of "upscale hippies," and local business types. It was definitely the cool place to be.

I entered the café at the far end to find the usual chaotic atmosphere of customers trying to order and others waiting to pick up their 100% organic meals. I remembered the time I overheard the owner say that the chaos was deliberate, to make it seem busy. I was surprised to find that what had seemed to be the height of inefficiency was actually cold, calculated marketing.

I leaned against the counter and saw that my lunch date Ted had just arrived. My heart caught. *Wow, he's just as handsome as I remember.* He stooped over a booth to speak with some diners, his tall frame towering over them. After waiting a few moments for him to come over, I grabbed a menu and pretended to be studying it. He eventually broke away and greeted me, clasping my hand in his huge bear paw.

"Geva, hi. Nice to see you. I've never been here before." He was smiling. "Do we order here or outside?" he said smiling.

"Right here," I said, pointing to the chaos. After we got our food, we made our way outside and found an empty table. I chose a seat facing the café so that he would be facing the uninteresting back of the restaurant. I wanted his full attention on me and on what I had to say.

"Ted, I'm glad you had time to for lunch. I wanted to tell you about the new evaluation services we've added to the company." I described how I had recently brought on an evaluation expert and that together we would be able to serve both nonprofits and foundations.

As we talked, I tried to focus on business but I was distracted by his blue eyes and beautiful lips. His tall frame was folded into the little café chair, crumpling his well-cut suit. The suit was fitting for the director of a major foundation. His face was angular and could have been chiseled out of marble, but his eyes held a weary sadness, probably related to the terrible divorce he had been through recently.

I had done business with Ted in the past when he was the grant administrator for his foundation and I was the grant manager for a nonprofit. He had struck me as incredibly intelligent then, always asking the right questions and always interested in the underlying aspects of any situation.

Our conversation now was restricted to our common interest of serving the community but I wondered what it would be like to spend time with someone as smart, compassionate and successful as him. *I bet we could have some really interesting conversations.* I started picturing hanging out with him on the weekends, probably at a really nice house, just relaxing and talking about the most interesting things...

"Well, it sounds great," he was saying. "You know I'm a big fan of evaluation. The new services will really help a lot of nonprofits around here make a greater impact on the community..."

I felt a little dizzy and tried to keep my thoughts on business. We were from two different worlds. His was composed of socialites and jets and parties, parties where the dinners cost more than my rent for a year. Mine was a constant struggle to help my nonprofit clients find better ways to do business and to access the funds they desperately needed. In ways we were on the opposite sides of the spectrum – he giving out the funding and I (and my clients) requesting it.

"You know Ted, most nonprofits can't afford evaluation. That's where the foundation could really help out. And it's in the best interest of the foundation to know whether the nonprofits are fulfilling their obligations." I wasn't feeling encouraged by this meeting.

"Well, I will definitely keep it in mind," he said. He was certainly not promising anything definite. I really wanted to take the conversation to a more personal level, but it just didn't feel right. And he didn't go there.

At the end of the meal he said, "What a great place to have lunch. I always end up eating at stuffy, upscale places like the Ritz," he said, looking around with a smile. Of course, it hadn't occurred to me to meet anywhere else. I always did business there. *Different worlds,* I thought.

"You've got to start hanging out with the cool kids, Ted," I said with a grin. We said our goodbyes and promised to keep in touch.

Chapter Twenty-three
Koreshan State Park

On the weekend, I decided to go to Koreshan State Park to practice spending time alone. I was looking forward to drawing in my new sketch book and being out in nature. I had always wanted a sketch book with a hard black cover and spiral binding when I was a teenager, but we could never afford extra things like that. I didn't even bother asking. But, now I was an adult, and I deserved a sketchbook. I happily stuffed the new sketch book in my messenger bag, along with some art supplies and set off.

At the park, I walked through the pines. Soft, brown needles carpeted the path. I passed picnic tables with families contentedly grilling burgers and made my way to the nature trails along the Estero River. I had been to the park several times with other people and various groups, but never by myself.

It felt different to be there alone, like I could really experience the place. It felt very... real. I walked slowly, taking in the different fragrances that rose up along the sandy trail. Somehow, I had all but lost my sense of smell some ten years prior, coinciding with my move to Florida. *Maybe it's the humidity down here*. But I could always smell scents on the air at Koreshan. I loved how the different smells came out of nowhere alternately spicy and woody, and then suddenly deeply floral. I tried to take them all in as I moved along.

Around me the vegetation of the forest intruded onto the sandy path, surrounding and engulfing it. Every now and then, other visitors would pass by with a smile and a greeting. Everyone seemed to be in a good mood, and I didn't mind seeing them. It was a shared experience. *This place belongs to all of us*, I thought.

I was looking for the perfect setting for drawing, passing by several potential spots before arriving at a grove of bamboo trees. The bright green shoots reached up to the sky and shaded the area in a canopy of tiny leaves. People had carved their names and thoughts into the bottoms of the trunks, which was both sad and kind of cool. I liked to see the comments from years ago.

I sat by the shore of the river, surrounded by bamboo trees. The spot was blanketed with soft, dried bamboo leaves to sit on and was secluded but still visible from the trail. I had brought a palette of water colors along and a bottle of water. I took out the sketchbook and flipped to an open page.

Looking around, I decided to paint the bamboo next to me. I was working on capturing the vibrant green of the trees, when a woman and boy walked by remarking "What a wonderful spot for painting!" I smiled and agreed.

I tried to capture the heart on the bamboo trees that read "J+H" in white, wondering who J and H were, and if they were still together. Did they still love each other?

Insects buzzed, and a breeze stirred the leaves. Kayakers passed by in the water and waved. I waved back, contentedly. I enjoyed painting the joints in the bamboo, where the trees stretched and grew.

I was growing hungry, and regretted not bringing a lunch with me. I stopped painting and just sat for a while, taking in the scenery. As more people passed by, my hunger got the best of me and I decided to call it a day. It wasn't a very long session, but I had successfully spent time alone and enjoyed myself painting.

***

As I drove along the long, dirt road to Happehatchee, I could hear the drumming already. The workshop was to be held in the gazebo where the yoga usually took place. I stopped by the main cottage and borrowed a drum. When I arrived at the gazebo, there were all kinds of people sitting in a semi-circle with drums in front of them. Jeanie greeted me and I grabbed a chair and settled in.

A girl named Cheri Shanti from Colorado led the weekend-long workshop, called "Evolution of the Drum Circle Community." When I saw it advertised in the Happehatchee newsletter, I thought it sounded intriguing, but I wasn't sure I was interested in the whole weekend. *I'll just check it out,* I had thought.

"My mission is to stimulate the remembrance of truth and authenticity in as many people as I possibly can," Cheri was saying. She was wearing a tight cotton top and leather shorts. She walked slowly around the room tapping a drum in time with her words. "I believe that when we get real with ourselves, then, and only then, can we accept 'what is' with the warriorship... and the conscious awareness necessary to create effective, evolutionary change, in ourselves, our community and our world."

She went on to talk about how she travels all over the world giving workshops and learning about drumming. "I believe that finding yourself and becoming 100% authentically alive is one of the biggest gifts we can give to the world." As she spoke, I imagined her travelling around the world studying drumming with the master drummers and giving workshops to different groups. It sounded like a lot of fun. *That's what I want to do,* I thought. *If she can work internationally, so can I.*

"Drum circles are communities," she said. "Drum circles can be dysfunctional or healthy depending on how much thought and intention is put into creating the space." The idea she said was to make a space where everyone feels like they are a part of the whole, where individuals don't take over and drown out the other musicians, and where everyone is contributing to a central rhythm.

"One way to do this," she told us "is to physically manipulate the circle, so that the larger drums are at the center with the strongest drummers close to them, so that they can hear the central beat and each other. The other drummers fan out from there, creating a V shape, instead of a circle." As she was describing this new configuration, I looked around and saw a variety of reactions. Jeanie looked enthusiastic but a couple of the drummers looked skeptical. I wondered if it would be possible to implement this new formation.

As she was talking, Cheri shared a few rhythms she had learned in Puerto Rico and Cuba. "Da da... da da, da da" she said as she tapped. I still felt awkward. "Da da...da da, da da." I felt like I was a step behind everybody else, just slightly off-beat.

"A lot of the African beats are actually six time rhythm rather than the four time rhythm that is popular in the United States. That's why it sounds so different to our ears." Finally I started to catch on. *Hey, I think I'm getting it!* I thought...until she started a new beat and I was back at square one. Sometimes I caught the rhythm, and sometimes I didn't. I tried not to be too hard on myself.

"There is a communication that happens between the dancers and the drummers," Cheri was saying. "Dancing is traditionally part of drum circles." In the videos I had seen there were always dancers moving to the music of the drums. "And it's very important to support the dancers. They get out there and open themselves up. It's a very vulnerable space for them. Sometimes dancers get into an ecstatic state and if the music changes abruptly it can profoundly affect them," Cheri said. I didn't really care. I wasn't interested in dancing. I just wanted to drum.

Some of the drummers in the room were quite good, and Cheri's instruction seemed to bring out the best in them. By the end of the workshop, I was enthusiastic both about creating community through drumming, and also about drumming in general.

***

Journal Entry: 3-25-2012

Yesterday, Bobbie Lee, the yoga instructor, said I looked radiant. She said I always look that way and that one day when she passed me on the long driveway to Happehatchee, I looked illuminated. I was really surprised by this and wondered if it has to do with the experiment. I don't think people have described me that way in the past.

Chapter Twenty-four
Do I Have to Get Married?

In the interest of research, I picked up a book called *Why Women Shouldn't Marry*, written by Cynthia S. Smith, first released in 1988. The second edition, updated 20 years later, was co-written by Smith and her daughter, Hillary B. Smith. It had always seemed like our entire culture was built on the concept that women have to marry, and I wanted to see what the counter-argument might be.

Cynthia Smith is a widow and Hillary is a divorced, single mom raising a son. The book examines both the cultural and personal implications of choosing not to marry, using interviews with women and anecdotes from their own lives. In the book Smith and her daughter challenge predominant social attitudes. For example, the Smiths suggest that "Most of the giving and compromising involved in marriage is performed by the women. Why do we need that? Is it because we have been socialized (or brainwashed) to believe we have more to gain from the arrangement and therefore must suppress our desires and sublimate our needs in order to make him happy?"

The Smith's thesis is that women should really examine their own underlying beliefs around marriage. *Why do we think we need to be married?* The Smiths point out that in the past, marriages were "functional partnerships." In the intense struggle of life, marriages were

147

arranged, based on financial stability and social status. Gradually, women began to choose their own spouses, but women still predominantly chose spouses based on their ability to provide. "Since the beginning of time, women have been driven into marriage by fears of their own inadequacies, which require the ministrations and care of men in order to survive."

But paradoxically, it seems that although women of the feminist era gained many freedoms, they retained some of the earlier programming. Although women have made significant strides professionally, "the burden carried by all of these women was that deep down, they still wanted the June Cleaver life - the husband, the 2.5 kids, and the house in the suburbs - as they had been brought up to desire. Sure, now they could buy the house themselves, but these educated, worldly women found they still had a foot in the prefeminist life and for the most part wanted children and fathers to live in the house with them. For that, they needed husbands, and that was when all the rhetoric of feminism came crashing down."

Oh My God! I thought. *That is so true! Regardless of the gains of the sixties we still think we need a man to be successful and happy.* Today, women can fully support themselves financially, and the pendulum has swung from "How much misery do I have to accept to keep him, to - how much happiness does he provide to make giving up my freedom worthwhile?"

One important concept the Smiths tackle is that of the "Soul Mate Myth," which stems from Greek mythology. The myth goes that Zeus became angered by the bold behavior of humans and decided to punish them by cutting them in half, which seemed like a good idea, but caused unforeseen complications. Thus, he decided to enable each half to come together with his or her respective other half. This sounds okay except for the obvious impracticalities such as the fact that one's soul mate might be located in another part of the world. It also creates an unrealistic set of expectations for a mate. He must be: a companion, a best friend, someone to talk to and support me, always there for me, ready to commit to me, someone who always puts me first, someone who loves me for who I am, and on and on...

Wow! This is why we think we're not enough. We have internalized the very myth that we are half a person. "Pursuing the soul mate myth with its constricting list of ideal qualities will lead to a woman staying single forever! But, more importantly, even if a woman locates a man who fulfills all of the qualities on the checklist, the Soul Mate myth creates unrealistic expectations for future performance. No one stays the same and the man who fits the bill today may change and become someone different in the future, something the myth doesn't take into account."

The Smiths presented a strong case for not marrying. I started reading the book to try to understand the background of the experiment, the big picture. But in my head it was starting to get personal. *I never really considered not ever marrying. That never even seemed like an option. Hmmm... the experiment was supposed to last a year and then I was supposed to go back to dating, a new and improved Geva. This research presents another option. I don't know if being single forever is for me, but...*

Chapter Twenty-five
Guitars

April

I was sitting on the bench outside of Kirk's studio. He was late again. Ten minutes late. His current student looked like a ten-year old from my place outside the studio looking in. I always made a point to be on time, but Kirk seemed to have a loose relationship with the clock.

How can he run a business that way? I thought. *My lesson is only a half hour long anyway!*

When he finished a few moments later, he was all smiles ushering me into the little room.

"Geva Darlin', how're ya doin' today?" he asked.

"Fine." I said getting settled in one of the chairs. *At least he always tries to put me at ease.*

"Well, you look nice today. What are you all dressed up for?" he asked.

I looked down at regular work clothes on, a blouse and pearls with a navy blue skirt. "I just came from work. Nothing special. Thanks." He was wearing his usual jeans and black tee shirt.

He's clearly not used to teaching adults I thought. I took out the guitar, re-positioned myself and then took a deep breath.

"Okay, have you been practicing? I know it's hard with your schedule." he said looking up from the book.

"Well, um... yes... yes I did practice this week" I replied. After working hard all day, usually the last thing I wanted to do was more work.

"Just once?" he asked looking at me expectantly.

"Well, yes I think at least once." Was that stretching the truth? *I think I practiced once this week...*

"Okay, well where did we leave off in this book?" He started flipping the pages.

We went through some of the exercises, and then we moved on to the new chords. By this time, my stomach was in knots and my breathing shallow. I tried to perfect the sounds. Kirk patiently repositioned my fingers and encouraged me on. Because the lesson was only a half hour long, we moved on quickly.

"Let's try 'Sweet Home Alabama' again. You like that song, right?" He started writing out the chords again, but in a different way. For the life of me, I couldn't get it. It just didn't sound right and my ego bounced back and forth between wanting to prove I could do it alone and feeling like a complete loser. The walls of the little room seemed to be closing in on me. I took another deep breath and let it out slowly.

Kirk never gave up on me. "It's supposed to be fun, Geva. Are you sure you want to do this?"

"Well, maybe eventually it will be fun... I'm sure." I said, wondering if that was true. *Will it ever be fun?* The skateboarding incident flashed into my mind. At ten I was fascinated with skateboarding. All the kids had them. I asked for one for my birthday, but not just any skateboard, a really fancy expensive one. I was so thrilled when I received it that I immediately ran outside to try it.

Two other skateboarders were at the top of a hill. I joined them and positioned the skateboard to take off. I put my left foot on top and pushed off with my right. The skateboard immediately flew out from under me and suddenly I was flying through the air. I landed with a hard thud on my back. Standing up slowly, trying to get my breath back and wincing in pain, I headed home. My parents didn't seem to notice the end of my short skateboarding career.

Am I kidding myself? I looked at Kirk. He was looking at my quizzically. "Yes, I'm sure it will be fun... someday," I said.

I can do this. I know I can.

"I'll try to practice more Kirk." I really meant it.

We finished the lesson and I walked out, Kirk passing his next student who was waiting patiently on the bench, ten minutes late for his lesson.

***

Mary had set up several appointments for me with ghostwriters but none of them seemed quite right. They were either under-qualified, over-qualified or just not quite right. Finally, I found what looked like the perfect fit. Mary arranged a lunch appointment with a gentleman I had come across on the library's website. The picture in the ad showed a white-haired man standing in the middle of a room that was filled with other white-haired, retired-looking people. The men were in polo shirts and the ladies had short hair. They all seemed to be smiling.

When I arrived at the restaurant that Mary had chosen, I recognized the author at the front door. We shook hands, and he introduced me to his wife/business partner. I was a bit taken aback, as I wasn't aware that anyone else was invited to the meeting. We found a booth around the back of the restaurant and started to discuss the project.

"Well Geva, I'm certainly glad you had time to meet up with us today. We're looking forward to hearing all about your book," Wayne said, clasping and unclasping his hands in front of him. "Let me tell you a little about how we work so that we can see if it's a good fit." He looked over at his wife for a moment before continuing.

"First I meet with the client and have a discussion about what they're trying to achieve with the project. Then, Marilyn meets with you and interviews you. She tape records the whole thing," he said, motioning to his wife, a gray haired woman in a white blouse with black buttons.

"Next, I sit down and write the text, and perhaps ask you some more questions. Over a period of several months, the book is written. Finally, my graphic designer, (who is also my daughter) will work on the cover."

"Okay, that sounds great," I said, imagining the process.

"Can you tell us a little about the book?" Wayne asked.

"Well, I'm not comfortable about telling too much about it at this point," I said looking at them. I didn't want anyone to grab the idea and publish a book about it before I had a chance to. "It's about an experiment that I conducted, which took place over the course of a year."

"What kind of experiment?" Marilyn said looking a little skeptical.

"Well, again, I can't go into it too much. But, I can say that it has to do with personal growth." Marilyn looked like she had bit down on a lemon when I said "personal growth."

"I don't understand," she said, "Is this a memoir?"

"Yes, it's a one-year period of my life. I conducted an experiment... and actually it's not even over yet, but I need to write about it." I told her.

With that Marilyn scowled, as if the concept of personal growth was not only foreign, but extremely distasteful to her.

"Well, that's okay," Wayne said. "We don't need to know everything at this point. I can see that it's a highly personal subject and you can tell us when you're ready."

If I wasn't so surprised by Marilyn's reaction, I would have felt sorry for her. She obviously lived in a very small world, and the idea of personal growth seemed to challenge her sensibilities.

Just then the waiter came up to the table. "What can I get you this afternoon?" he said in a Spanish accent.

Wayne and Marilyn were still looking at the menu. "I'll have a cheeseburger, medium rare," Wayne said.

Marilyn was still looking at her menu. I handed mine to the waiter without opening it. "I'll have an omelet with spinach, mushrooms and Swiss cheese, and a side of potatoes.

"I want a Cobb salad. I don't see it," she said, turning the menu over and over. "I want the one with the meat on top."

"Yes, ma'am we don't have a cobb salad. We only have a house salad. Is that fine?"

"Yes, the one with the meat on top," she said handing him the menu. *This is not going to go well,* I thought.

When I asked what the price range was for their services, Wayne talked in circles and was never specific. Then he pulled out a folder and said, "If you decide you want to move forward with us, this is the contract." And with that he began to discuss the contract. I thought, *What kind of alternate universe have I suddenly stepped into? Here he is discussing a contract at the first meeting and I haven't even heard the price...*

Just then the waiter walked up and laid down my omelet, Wayne's cheeseburger and Marilyn's house salad. "Hey, I asked for a..." she said, her voice trailing after the waiters back as he walked away. I tried to stifle my amusement.

"Wayne, I can't talk to you about a contract without knowing the price, or at least a range," I said cutting into the omelet. Marilyn was grimacing.

"Well," he said, looking over at his wife. "It depends on the project. Most of our clients are retired and... rather affluent, and what we are used to getting is in the neighborhood of $120,000," he said, looking me straight in the eye.

I almost fell off my chair. *Did I hear him right?* I tried not to let the shock show on my face.

"We understand that this is a different situation. You are still working. What can you afford?"

"Well, you know, I think I will have to give it some thought," I said. *I am so not interested in working with these strange people,* I thought.

After lunch, I told them I would be in touch, and made my way to the restroom. As I walked, I tried to let the strange events settle into my mind. *Seriously?... Seriously? $120,000 to ghost write a book?* I was glad the meeting was over and I could put those bizarre people behind me.

Leaving the bathroom stall, I noticed a girl at the sink, washing her hands. Usually, I would just wash my own hands and go about my business. I wouldn't notice this stranger's presence or take it into account. Instead, I looked up and said, "Hi." I just stood there and let her take her turn.

She turned to me and said, "You look nice today."

I was so surprised. "Thanks," I said as she left.

I looked in the mirror. I was just dressed for work. I did have my favorite strand of pearls on. *Hmmmmm.....* I thought. *In the past random strangers never complimented my appearance.* I turned and left puzzling over the encounter.

Chapter Twenty-six
Earth Day

When I arrived at Koreshan State Park there were cars lined up all the way to the street for the Earth Day Festival. I parked and headed toward the settlement side of the park. There were people milling around the various booths, but fewer people than I thought there would be.

I was looking for my parents' booth. They were selling their Moringa products. I wondered how sales were going, since there weren't many people walking around. They had started selling products made from the Moringa plant a few years prior, and were still struggling to make the business successful.

Moringa was supposed to be a miracle plant with the highest nutritional value of any plant in the world. I was wary. They had owned one small business after the other, and had expected my sisters and I to believe that each one was the answer to all our problems. Apparently, Moringa supplements are given to pregnant women in developing countries to increase birth weight and reduce mortality rates. And it very well could be the "ultimate plant," but I couldn't get the image of Jack's magic beans out of my head. I had bought enough snake oil from them over the years. *At least they never give up*, I thought. I did want to see them in their new booth, giving it a good try.

I made a loop of the park twice looking for the booth, but couldn't seem to find it. *I hope they picked a good location,* I thought.

Finally, in frustration I dialed their number. "Mom, where are you guys? I can't find your booth."

"Oh, I'm sorry honey. We're at home. We were just too tired this morning, so we decided not to come."

I couldn't believe it. I don't even like festivals. I probably wouldn't have come to the event if she hadn't invited me. "I see. Well, I'll talk to you later."

"I'm sorry, honey. We should have called you. Well, at least you can enjoy the festival."

"Yeah right. Whatever. I've got to go." *They are unbelievable*, I thought. *Not only were they too tired to work at their own business, but they didn't even call to tell me they had changed their minds.*

Well, at least I can go to the drum circle, I thought, and headed toward the Founder's House, where the drum circle was to be held. That side of Koreshan State Park was the site of a former cult compound. The Founder's House was one of the many buildings that the Koreshans had built on the 320 acre property. Its long porch wrapped around the brown, rough-hewn building.

I loved the Koreshans and their eclectic beliefs. I always felt like their ghosts were floating around the property, unseen. *I wonder if they approve of the Earth Day Festival on their property,* I thought. *I bet they did.* The Koreshans had seemed to have an intimate relationship

158

with the land and were a bit radical in their thinking. The ghosts probably enjoyed the celebration of the earth.

The founder, Cyrus Teed, was a physician who in 1869, suffered an electrical shock during an experiment which rendered him unconscious. While unconscious, he had a divine inspiration, causing him to believe that he was the messiah of a new religious belief. He changed his name to Koresh (Hebrew for Cyrus), and began spreading the beliefs of Koreshanity.

Teed began preaching his beliefs in New York, but his controversial religion caused tension, and they relocated to Florida in 1894. They built a village consisting of a bakery, printing house, the World College of Life, a general store, concrete works, a power plant, and multiple housing buildings.

I thought of the time I had brought my five year old niece on a tour of the settlement. She was very excited about the idea of a group of people creating their own community. She asked all sorts of questions about the Koreshans and their lifestyle.

The tenets of Koreshanity revolved around the core belief of Cellular Cosmogony. They believed the earth and universe were contained inside a sphere known as a cell. They spent much of their time conducting science experiments, in attempts to prove this theory. They also believed in reincarnation, immortality, alchemy, communal living and celibacy.

Teed was also a feminist. In his vision, he saw that God was half male and half female. As a result, Teed was a big proponent of women's rights. He even created a system of government in which eight women administered the cult. But inevitably, membership began to dwindle following Teed's death in 1908. *If they were still around, I probably would have been sucked right into their cult,* I thought, and smiled.

I arrived at the Founder's House. The drum circle wasn't supposed to start for another hour. Jeanie and Starbo were already setting up. She had on a long tie dyed skirt, a tank top and some kind of herbs pinned to the back of her long hair. "Hi Jeanie, how's it going?"

"Great, how are you?" she said.

"Good. Can I borrow a drum? I still don't have one."

"Sure, no problem. There's one on the porch," she said, pointing.

"Thanks," I said.

The circle was supposed be in the shade behind the founder's house. I walked over to a big tree to sit and wait. I recognized a guy leaning on the tree from the workshop with Cherie Shanti. I had seen him around. He was clearly older than me, but I couldn't tell by how much. He had a beard and mustache, and usually wore a baseball hat. I was curious about him. He always seemed so self-contained. He was a good drummer and seemed perfectly content to just play music and be by himself. *That's how I want to be*, I thought.

"Hi, how's it going?" I asked.

"Good. Are you here for the drum circle?" He looked at the drum in my arms.

"Yep. When is it supposed to start?"

"In an hour, I think. I'm George."

"Geva. Nice to meet you," I said, wondering what this drum circle would be like.

"How long have you been drumming?" I asked.

"Oh, forever. I play the guitar and banjo, too."

"Really? That's so cool. I'm learning the guitar now," I told him.

"Yeah? Are you taking lessons?" he said, looking up. He had kind eyes.

"Yes, but they're only a half hour long. It's not going too well so far."

"Are you practicing outside of the lessons?"

"Not really," I admitted down dejectedly.

"Well, we should hang out sometime, and practice," he said picking up his drum.

The awesomeness of the statement almost overwhelmed me. Some small part of me tried to say *Hey! Wait a minute. You are about to break the main rule of the experiment: no dating.* But the part of me that had always wanted to play the guitar and never had anyone to practice with promptly stomped on the nay-saying part's head.

"That would be awesome!" I said without hesitation.

"Yes, you need to practice for several hours at a time, not for just half an hour. You can't get anything done that way."

161

That would be so cool, I thought picturing myself practicing with someone who knew what they were doing.

"Just keep in mind, I'm no instructor." He chuckled.

We exchanged contact information and talked about setting up something during the next week. After a while, more people showed up and began setting up for the drum circle. *This should be interesting,* I thought. There were also non-drummers standing around waiting to see what a drum circle was all about.

Bill, one of the better drummers, came and set his drum down. I put my drum between his and Starbo's. It didn't occur to me that women aren't usually drummers. But when I looked around, I noticed that there were no women drumming around me. Jeanie was set up a few rows back. I was on the frontline. Somebody set up massive drums with a bell on top. The drumming began tentatively. Most drummers kept the main beat and several of the better drummers "soloed." Bill was a really intense, fast drummer and I struggled to keep up. Eventually, the rhythm increased in intensity, and I was able to blend in.

A few people came into the center of the circle, timidly, at first feet gently stamping in time to the beat. One woman began making fluid movements with her arms, while a young guy with a beard was popping up and down to the beat. A girl with long, blond hair danced with a baby on her hip and a toddler clinging to her leg. Bah bah bah, buh bah bah bah....Bah bah bah, buh bah bah bah...

More people moved into the middle and an electric rhythm started to take over. Bah bah bah, buh bah bah bah. I beat the drum in time as the dancers moved. Young, old, black, white, rich, poor, everyone moved separately and together creating an ecstatic feeling of celebration.

A light rain started to fall despite the sun overhead. Pretty soon it was almost body to body in the middle of the circle and people were cheering. The beat was tremendous and one guy started yelling, "Freedom! Freedom!" After an hour or so, feeling satisfied, I got up and made my way out. *Note to self: buy a drum.*

***

Journal Entry: 4-30-2012 Homelessness

I woke up in the middle of the night after a bad dream. In the dream I had been sitting on the side of the road behind a restaurant and fell asleep. When I woke up, my ex-husband Carlos was there, and I needed to decide what to order at the restaurant. I guess what bothered me was that it felt like the dream was about homelessness. I had been sitting on a curb, kind of like a homeless person.

I have been wrestling with my fear of homelessness recently. Ever since I was little, I had a fear of homelessness. We moved so many times that I never felt like anything was permanent and it seemed like devastation was around every corner. I can remember reading about homelessness in high school, and being intrigued by what a pervasive problem it was. I had a simultaneous interest in working on the problem and a fear of it.

But now it was my own potential homelessness that is waking me up in the middle of the night. I keep picturing the studio that my parents offered me. I have a fear that if I put everything in storage and leave the condo, chaos will break out and I will end up homeless. One reassuring fact is that I have done this before - When I went to Kripalu for the spiritual retreat, when I went to India for two months and when I lived in Mexico for five months while waiting for Carlos' visa. Each time I put my things in storage and gave up a home.

I guess the thing that bothers me is that my parents have the threat of foreclosure hanging over them. That doesn't seem like a good foundation to rely on.

Chapter Twenty-seven
Seriously?

May

I was staring at the email in disbelief. I had requested folders in January from Brad's assistant, Michelle. It was now May, and I had written her again to see if they had arrived. She wrote back "Geva, you were here yesterday. You could've picked them up. Lisa has enough mailing to bring to the other side that I won't ask her to bring those folders to you and I'm not going over there just to bring you the folders. We ordered a bunch a long time ago and I remember telling you we had them. We have a lot that already have stickers on them. You can reuse them. Just ask Kate to print you a sticker to put on top of the other one. They're in my office."

I stewed on the situation for a few minutes, trying to decide whether to ignore her rudeness and simply, not reply at all, or to confront the situation head on. When construction began, they had moved the development function to a building a few streets away, which was a huge inconvenience since I supported that department.

I could not believe a secretary could be so rude. Yes, Michelle had been promoted to development assistant, but she was still the secretary for the department. The entire time I had been with the organization both as an employee and as a contractor, I had been disrespected. I was always walking on egg shells around everyone else's feelings. I thought of The 28 Laws of Attraction and "no tolerations" and wrote back "I wasn't aware of the need for the folders until after I had returned to the office yesterday, and I really don't appreciate your attitude."

Michelle replied "I'm sorry Geva but I don't appreciate yours either."

I wrote back "I really don't understand exactly what I've done wrong in this situation, but I would be happy to schedule a time to discuss it." This time I copied her supervisor on the email chain.

Fifteen minutes later she replied "Geva, I don't think we need a meeting to discuss this. We have enough work over here and everyone is very busy. I will never call you if I need something from our mailbox, a check or anything. If I need it, I come over and get it. You need the folders, you can certainly ask me if I ordered them. If the folders are here, you can stop by and pick them up. It's as simple as that. You did the same exact thing with the notecards, and I sent them to you before. Lisa is not a messenger, and she has enough on her plate. Don't we all? If this is something you need to do your job, don't wait for us to bring them to you. I hope you understand my reasons now."

I could not believe that she would speak to me this way. We had always been friends despite the fact that I clearly outranked her. Maybe she was embarrassed that she had been caught in an obvious mistake.

I waited to hear back from her supervisor, but did not hear back that day. The argument bothered me the whole rest of the day and into the evening. *I don't understand what I did wrong.* Brad always talked about roles and responsibilities. It was her role and responsibility to order supplies. It was not her place to tell me to reuse supplies or that I had to come pick them up myself. And it was Lisa's role to deliver mail back and forth. It didn't make sense.

She was probably resisting the idea that I outranked her, and was pushing back on that. But there had to be something else. Something about this interaction reminded me of the author's wife. It was as if they both were resentful of my ability to own my own power. Michelle had worked at the organization for longer than I had and during her time there I had had two promotions and then opened my own business. During that time, she struggled to start and finish a degree and still had not moved on. She and the author's wife were both like animals that were trapped in cages and my presence pointed out their slavery too clearly.

I still didn't understand how such a negative situation could arise so suddenly. I felt powerless to fix it and I waited for Brad's response. I was sure he would tell her that it was her role to support the department, and that I, as a contractor, did not have time to drive to their office to pick up supplies, which could easily be brought over. I was surprised that I didn't receive a response that day, nor the following day, a Friday. Over the weekend the situation bothered me off and on.

On Monday, I had a regularly scheduled meeting with Brad in his office. I closed the door and asked him about the emails and his reaction. I was surprised when he said "I've requested a meeting with both of you. I was very unhappy to see those emails flying back and forth."

"Okay..." I let the subject drop and moved on to something else. Over the next few days, I waited for a meeting request to arrive. It was an extremely busy time and the request never arrived.

Brad is one of the most diplomatic people I know, and later, in a completely unrelated meeting he said something that struck a chord with me. He was talking about an incident he had with a donor. "Sometimes, you have to see the bigger picture in relationships, and apologize for something that may not have even been your fault. The relationship is the most important thing."

His words hit home and I started to think about my friendship with Michelle. We had been friends for such a long time. How could I let something so stupid ruin it? And I needed her help frequently. Should I jeopardize that simply for the sake of being right?

I left Brad's office and walked down to Michelle's, feeling sure I was about to do the right thing. "Hi Michelle," I said walking in. She looked up from her computer, surprise registering on her face. Before she could say anything, I said "Listen I'm really sorry about the misunderstanding we had."

Her face instantly softened from agitated surprise to calm and open. "Thank you, Geva. You have to understand that Lisa makes several trips a day over to the main office and she has to carry that big bin from the post office."

"Yeah, I know. It's a pretty big bin," I said, picturing the bin.

"And it's really heavy. I can't ask her to carry a box of folders on top of that," she said looking tired. I could kind of see her point. Everybody was overworked there. But, the main thing to do was to repair the relationship.

168

"Yes, I understand now," I said. We chatted for a few more minutes, catching up, and I left the office feeling better. Brad was right. Relationships are the most important thing.

The whole situation reminded me of the fight I had with Suzanne Pimpiano in the 9th grade. I had moved to Avon, New York, the summer before and Suzanne and I were just becoming friends. Sometimes she rode my bus and we would sit together, although most of the time she got a ride with one of her many friends. She was pretty and cool and one of the most popular girls in the school, I just struggled to get by socially. I was thrilled that Suzanne would even talk to me.

I can't remember what the conversation was even about, but I remember sitting at a big, round table in the library with a bunch of Suzanne's friends. I remember that I was kind of showing off, not used to being included in a group like that. There was some sort of misunderstanding related to Suzanne and I remember one of the girls saying "Well, are you going to apologize to Suzanne?"

I remember feeling like the conversation was spinning wildly out of control. I blurted out, "She can apologize to me." There was a shocked silence. One girl whispered to another and then the table kind of dispersed. I didn't know what to do. There was no one I could talk to in order to get advice. My parents were busy with their own problems and never asked about my life anyway. I hoped the problem would resolve itself on its own somehow.

I waited to see what Suzanne would say, but, she just ignored me. It was as if I had never existed. She looked the other way in the halls and when she rode the bus, she sat far away. The next two years of high school were definitely challenging. I spent a lot of time alone, and was sometimes the object of derision by some patently mean kids.

Apparently, as an adult, I still really did not know how to manage relationships or resolve conflict. *Note to self: learn how to solve conflicts better.*

Chapter Twenty-eight
Changes

That Friday, the president's assistant stuck her head in the door of the office to say   "Oh, by the way, they're coming to move your office on Monday."

"What? You've got to be kidding me," I said, staring at her in shock.

"No, I'm pretty sure they're coming on Monday and your function will be in the development building," she said. I had known about the move for a while, but thought for sure it would be at least another month before it happened. I grabbed a few boxes and started filling them with files and mementos. I packed as much as I could and then went back to work at the computer.

The thought of moving to the development building was the last straw. I couldn't take it. I had been at the organization for six years. I had been through so much there. But I couldn't imagine sharing an office with Michelle and the rest of the development team, a bunch of back-biting women.

I thought about it that afternoon and on my way to Brad's office for our previously scheduled meeting. Now was the time to make a clean break. I was planning to replace myself with someone on my company's team but that would mean at least six months of training her. I literally didn't think I could take a single day more. Brad and I were supposed to discuss a few grants at the meeting, but when I came in, I started by asking if I could close the door.

"Brad, I know we had discussed my replacing myself with Rene, but I just don't think that is going to work. I think we should make a clean break." Brad looked taken aback.

"What's brought this on?" He looked shocked and a little panicked.

"Well, I just have other things I want to do, and I'm feeling a bit under-appreciated around here."

"I'm sorry you feel that way." He still looked shocked. "Is there anything we can do to change your mind?" he said still looking surprised.

"I don't think so," I said, settling into the chair.

"What kind of a timeframe are you thinking about? When are you anticipating a last day?"

"As soon as possible. Probably two weeks," I said meeting his gaze.

"Well, let's talk about transitioning your work load. Obviously, we will have to shift some things around and possibly put some things off."

Brad and I worked out a transition plan, discussing which projects were priorities, which were less urgent, and who could take over which project.

"I'm sorry you feel under-appreciated. I think you've always done good work. Are you sure you don't want to think about it over the weekend?" *Well, if he's going to give me an out, I'm going to take it*, I thought.

"Sure, I'll think about it over the weekend." We set an appointment for late Monday morning, and I said goodbye. I walked out without saying goodbye to anyone in the office.

Outside, in my car I thought, *Okay, this experiment is getting out of hand. Suddenly, my whole life is changing...* I looked down at my phone. There was an email informing me that Happehatchee was closing for two months. I felt the floor fall out from under me. I sat there trying to take in the shock. I knew I had made the right decision about work, but it seemed that Happehatchee was more important to me than I realized. I didn't know how much I had counted on it being there, supporting me.

Suddenly, part of my support structure was gone. I knew it would be closed for more than two months. They were so disorganized. I called Jeanie, and she confirmed that the board had voted to close Happehatchee for a while. I was suddenly unemployed and had no special place to back me up. *Oh my God! Okay, take a deep breath,* I thought. *How am I going to find more work? And quickly? Okay, calm down,* I said to myself. *One step at a time. Build on what you have.*

I thought about the concept of over-responding from The 28 Laws of Attraction. Instead of just managing a situation, you try to go beyond and completely take care of it. I immediately went out and spent $500 on a car repair and then another $175 on a new car stereo. The car repair was necessary and the car stereo took it a step beyond. I wanted to make a commitment to moving forward. I had ordered French tapes and the old stereo was broken. Now, I would be able to listen to them.

After the "investments" I made, not only did I feel like I had solid transportation to get wherever I needed to go, but I felt a little more steady, a little more in control. And because of the investment in the car stereo, a feeling of abundance was returning. Somehow it would work out. I had taken care of myself. I had invested in my present and my future. I didn't know what the future would look like, but I had solid transportation and Paris was in my future.

I thought about the work situation over the weekend. It had been six years. I was ready to move on. And I definitely didn't want to move into the other building. The women who worked in that office were just not my style. They seemed very rigid, cold and petty. And I would have had to spend at least six months there, training my replacement. Six long months…

That's when Irene came to mind. She was a grant writer on my team of consultants, and was even more qualified to do the job than Rene. Irene's side job was finishing up in a few weeks, so she might be able to pick the job up immediately. I had already begun training Rene, but she would have to understand. When I called Irene, she agreed immediately.

On Monday when I met with Brad, I explained that I had thought it over and come up with another plan. I outlined the idea of having Irene take my place, with me staying involved on a strategic level.

"Well, that sounds possible but I would have to meet Irene, he said. He looked relieved at the thought of not having to find a replacement. And as it turned out, the move to the new building was postponed. I headed out to lunch feeling like I had done what I had to do. As I drove to the café across town, I tried not to think about the implications of the decision I'd made. I knew that whatever happened next could only be positive. *Maybe I should stop at the fun little jewelry store by the café after lunch.*

I was making my way around the salad bar when I saw Kevin, a guy I had dated briefly six months prior. *Oh, geez...* What had started out so promising, ended up quite a disappointment. He was smart and interesting with a sarcastic sense of humor, but sometime between our first and second date, he lost his job. Which wouldn't have bothered me, but it really threw his life into turmoil. He had moved in with his sister and stopped calling me. I tried not to take it personally, but it had bothered me. When I saw him in the café, my heart raced and my palms got sweaty.

I quickly put together a salad, paid the cashier and made my way to the little dining area. *Maybe I can eat fast and get out of here,* I thought. There were only about eight tables and two of them were taken. I sat down and tried not to be obvious as I peeked over the railing to see if he was around. Suddenly, I heard, "Geva, hey there. How are you?"

I looked up to see his smiling face.

"Kevin, hi." I wondered if he had seen me peeking around.

"Would you like company for lunch?"

"Uh, sure," I said, making room.

Over lunch, he told me how his life had improved over the last six months. He had found a job and his life was stabilizing.

"Yes, it's really good. I really like it at the hospital," he said in his New York accent.

"That's great. Have you been having any fun?"

175

"Well, not really. I'm still trying to finish my degree. I study a lot." *What did I see in him again?* He was still handsome, but not much fun. I shared with him some of the exciting things I had been up to. I thought about the experiment and the no dating vow.

"I'm sorry, I've got to get going," I said apologizing. "I've got some shopping to do."

"Can we keep in touch?" He looked crestfallen.

"Of course. It was nice to see you. Take good care."

I was walking across the parking lot to the jewelry store when I received his text asking if I had the same number. I ignored it and continued on to the jewelry store. Looking at all the pretty necklaces and bracelets, I thought about Kevin and his text. I didn't want to respond right away. I left without buying anything. When I got back to the office I replied that the number was correct, wondering what this meant.

Over the next few weeks, I introduced Irene to Brad and began negotiating. I drafted a contract for his consideration. The compensation was fair all around. Because they weren't paying taxes or benefits, the total amount of the contract was less than what they had been paying for my full salary. If accepted, I would still be earning money on the new contract, but not nearly as much as before. I wondered how that would affect my lifestyle. I had some savings, but didn't like the idea of spending it down.

Chapter Twenty-nine
Apartment Hunting

When I walked through the door of my spacious, light-filled condo that evening, I thought about my new income level. In reality, I couldn't afford to rent such an expensive place. It worked at the higher income level, now, maybe not. *Do I really need to live in a community with a pool, tennis courts and a fitness center? Maybe I should just find an interim step, someplace less expensive, and less of a commitment, a place that would allow me to travel and move around, something a little more flexible.*

I started combing through online ads for efficiencies and rooms for rent. The first place I looked at was a little efficiency off a garage. The property was definitely missing a woman's touch with a scraggle of weeds and shrubs. I grew up in the country. *It's not that bad...* I almost talked myself into it, but there was no room to do yoga and the driveway was a mess. The owner had dumped all these pieces of red tile down on the unpaved, circular drive. It looked ridiculous, like some hillbilly hideout. I would save almost $500 a month, but I just couldn't see it. I couldn't see living there. I didn't care if it was temporary. *Living here would definitely bring me down.*

The next place was a big, beautiful house on a canal. The room available was small and painted a shocking-blue color. The owner was a guy in his forties who seemed to keep odd hours. The clincher was the dead moose's head on the wall. Very bad karma. *Couldn't possibly live there.* I saw an ad for an efficiency about 10 minutes north of where I was living. When I drove into the community I felt immediately at home. The street had old trees and a comfortable, relaxed feel. When I knocked on the door, the owner came out smiling and showed me around to the efficiency.

I felt relaxed as soon as I walked through it. There was a large airy, bedroom, with a bathroom off the side. The only drawback was the kitchen. It wasn't a real kitchen. There was a sink and a small refrigerator next to the entrance, but no stove. There was a sort of camp stove set up with two burners. Across from this, was the washer and dryer. The owner said he also used them, meaning that he came into the space frequently. There wasn't even room for a table. We talked for a few minutes, and I contemplated whether I could live without an actual kitchen.

"What do you do for work?" he asked.

"I own a small business here in southwest Florida," I replied. He looked down as I was describing the business, obviously put off by the fact that I didn't have a traditional job. *Maybe he thinks small business owners are unreliable...*I thought.

"Um, I guess I'll think it over and get back to you," I said, and shook his hand.

The next day, my thoughts kept coming back to the efficiency. *Could I live without a functioning kitchen?* I could picture spending time in the bedroom and bathroom. *What about the owner coming in to use the washer and dryer?* I kept going back and forth in my head. Kevin texted me, but I ignored it. Finally, around 7 p.m., it occurred to me that I might be able to put a real stove in at my own expense if the owner would be open to it. I decided to give him a call.

"Hi, this is Geva. I came to look at the efficiency yesterday. I was-"

"I'm sorry," he interjected. "It's been rented."

"Oh, okay thanks," I said and hung up.

I sat there wondering if I should have acted faster. One of the principles in the 28 Laws of Attraction is to not only "overrespond" to situations but also to act immediately. For the rest of the week, I tried, but couldn't find any housing worth looking at. I came across a house to share that was in a good location, but the owner mentioned that he usually spent the whole weekend at home. I made an appointment to see it but eventually cancelled. I didn't want to spend that much time with anyone.

Journal Entry: 4-24-2012 Eye of the Hurricane

I feel like I'm going through the eye of the hurricane. I'm trying not to let my fears get the best of me. Nothing seems to be coming together - at least not the way I thought it would. The organization is dragging its feet. We're negotiating for Irene to replace me, and now they want a substantial training period. No alternate living arrangements seem to be opening up.

I decided that I needed to get a better idea of how much space I would need, so I organized my garage. Almost all of my personal belongings were stored there because I'd rented my condo furnished. The boxes were strewn about haphazardly, some open, some without tops. I spent the better part of a morning going through them and stacking them at the back of the garage.

I filled eight boxes with books that I no longer needed and loaded them in the car. The local library agreed to take them and after heaping their carts, I took off like a bandit. *My load is getting lighter.* Back at the condo, I surveyed the garage, confident in the amount I had to move. I still wasn't sure I was going to be able to move into a single room. I might need to rent some additional storage space.

Then one day when I was on the phone with my mother and she mentioned that a friend of hers was looking to rent half of her house. I knew Pam and thought it might be a possibility. I had never particularly liked Pam, but I didn't dislike her. She and my mother had been friends for years, and she had attended several family events.

Pam seemed like a frivolous woman. Although she liked art and collected it, there didn't seem to be any depth to her. She held parties at her Naples house to which I was invited but I generally declined. The few times I had attended no one had anything interesting to say. But for some reason my mom really liked Pam. *Who knows*, I thought. *She's probably harmless and at least I know her. It's worth a look.*

Her house was a ranch-style home in a suburban neighborhood in Bonita Springs. Pam, a short somewhat round woman with close-cropped hair, met me at the door. "Geva, how are you? I haven't seen you in ages." As she made way for me to pass, I could see that she had brought a lot of the decorations from her Naples home. There were two large antique travel posters from Cuba on the opposite wall.

"Well, good. Yes, I've been doing really well. Thanks," I replied, looking around. To my left were two sitting areas with crazy leopard print leather couches. Two small white dogs yapped at her feet. *Hmmm, I'm not a huge fan of dogs but at least they're small.*

"Your mom tells me you're looking to share a place."

"Yes, I want to do some travelling and I want a little less commitment." I reached down to pet the dogs.

"Well, that sounds fine. I'm actually planning on doing a bit of travelling myself. And, you know I still have the Naples house. I rent that for the winter months. But other than that I'll be gone and you'd have the house to yourself," she said. *I like the sound of that.*

Would you like a tour?" she asked smiling. We made our way through the house.

"There are two rooms available," she said, pointing to a separate wing off the living room. I walked past her and down the hall. *A separate wing. Awesome.*

Both rooms had creamy, yellow-colored walls, always a good sign. I loved that color for walls. The rooms were separated by a bathroom with marble tile and a deep pedestal sink. The first room would make a great combination office and living room, and it was big enough to do yoga in.

The second room already had a bed in it and would make a fine bedroom. Both rooms had huge, double closets. The wall to wall carpeting gave the rooms a cozy feel. She was asking more than I had planned on spending, but

181

because it was for two rooms, I agreed. "I'll take it," I said, confidently. The rental would start June 15th.

***

Journal Entry: 5-21-2012 Foreclosure

I can't believe that one day after I finally find a place, I find out that my parents' house is really going to be foreclosed. I have been worrying and wondering what they're going to do.

Kevin keeps texting me every week. The other night he texted "You should be at Music Walk with me." I'm not sure whether I would prefer that he give up and leave me alone so I can focus on my life, or whether I would prefer that he stay in touch over the next four and a half months. I guess I would prefer that he leave me be, and then get in touch after the four and a half months are over. I texted him saying "I can't do anything until October." He didn't respond.

Thinking about Kevin doesn't occupy my time the way it would have in the past. There is always so much more to think about, so much more to do these days. My time is always filled. If there's nothing scheduled, I should be practicing either the guitar or the drum.

Chapter Thirty
Drum Circle

I was headed to the drum circle in Fort Myers, which met each Sunday at 6 pm. As I drove, I wondered what it would be like. Several people told me that I should try out the Fort Myers drum circle, because it was the best one in the area. As I approached the park, I couldn't hear anything. I pulled in under the underpass, and looked for the group.

Off to my left, I saw some people in a group of chairs, by the side of the river. I could barely make out the sound of drumming. *Was this a bad idea? I wondered.* I had mixed feelings about the whole thing. I had really enjoyed drumming at Happehatchee and on Earth Day, but there seemed to be some stigma attached to drum circles. *What kind of people went to them, and why? The weirdos? the odd balls? the misfits?*

As I stepped out of the car, I tried to clear my mind and be open to whatever happened. I pulled my big, new drum from the backseat, and started walking. I saw George, who waved as I approached. There was a slow, steady rhythm playing and I recognized a few familiar faces. I set up my chair and drum between a guy with long hair and faded blue jeans and a woman with short, dark hair. She smiled and kept drumming.

Across the way, I noticed Jeanie and Starbo drumming. There was quite a variety of people actually: a woman with two little children playing at her feet; several older people who looked kind of middle class; a big woman in a colorful dress with bright blond hair; a young Hispanic guy; a slightly plump guy playing congas and a woman with short red hair dancing in the middle. They all seemed very relaxed.

I tried to get into the rhythm. I made several mistakes on the drum, but nobody seemed to notice. Between rhythms the woman next to me said "Hi, I'm Paula."

"I'm Geva," I said.

"Have you been here before?" she asked.

"No, this is my first time."

"Oh, well welcome. Welcome to the group." she said smiling. "This is Jim," she said motioning to the middle-aged man next to her.

"Howdy," he said with a wave.

As the sun began to set, I started getting into the rhythm and was able to keep up. Jeanie danced in the middle of the circle making slow wavelike movements with her arms. *Boy, is she brave*, I thought. *I want to be like that.* I couldn't imagine dancing alone in front of a group. At the end of the night I said goodbye to Paula and Jim.

"Hey, great to meet you! See you next week," Paula said. Jim smiled and waved.

As I drove away, I felt a quiet sense of fulfillment. I thought about the eclectic group creating rhythms under the stars. They seemed like a friendly group of people. *Maybe normal is over-rated anyway.*

Chapter Thirty-one
The Gypsy

June

Moving has always been stressful for me, in spite of the fact that I have moved 37 times. Twelve of those times were before I was ten years old. People always ask why my family moved so much, and I never have a good answer for them. In the early days, my parents were experimenting with alternative lifestyles (read: hippie, not gay). They had a leather goods store for four years, and we lived out in rural Pennsylvania. The local economy deteriorated and we moved up to New York, where we lived with my grandparents for a while.

We had barely settled into one house when the paperwork was approved for my Dad to start college. So we moved into the "married student housing" at the university. We lived on the campus for a couple years and then moved out to a small town in the country after my dad graduated. Eventually, my parents moved to Massachusetts where I finished high school.

Two weeks after graduation, I moved out on my own but I continued the pattern of moving every few years. There was always a good reason for it and it always seemed to relate to work or school in some way. The last few moves had been by choice. After a foreclosure in 2009, I moved to a better location. The next move was to a prettier condo in a better community.

This move to Pam's house was taking a risk because it was downsizing. *Am I moving forward or backward?* I could only hold on to faith that this move was in a positive direction, that I was trading the security of a big beautiful condo for freedom and growth.

I hate being not quite out of one home and not fully moved into the next one. The feeling of being unsettled, being in-between places, really irks me. Every few days I packed boxes into the car and drove them down to Pam's, stacking them against the garage wall. On Sunday, Matthew (Garan's husband) brought their van down to help me move the few pieces of furniture I was taking: two bookcases, a twin bed, a desk and a rocking chair.

We put the twin bed in the second room to use as a daybed. Mathew works a full-time job and is in the Marine Corps as a reservist, and as he helped me carry the heavy book shelves from the van to the house, I thought about how nice it was of him to take the time to come and help me. It was almost like having a brother.

On the final moving day, when I arrived at Pam's house, she told me that the air conditioning system had broken a few days before. She had hired an unlicensed HVAC guy, who kept promising to come and install a new system. "Pam, you know, sometimes saving money in the short run is not such a good thing in the long run." I was thinking of the 28 Laws of Attraction.

"What do you mean?" she asked.

"Well, working with unlicensed people can save you a few bucks, but if anything happens, your insurance won't cover it."

Several hot days went by and I had all the windows open. At night it was so hot that I had to bring a wash cloth to bed to cool my face and neck. The repairman finally showed up at 8:00 pm on Thursday, with his wife as assistant. Pam took one look at the weight of the AC unit and the ladder to the attic where the unit was to be installed and cancelled the whole thing. She ordered a new unit from a licensed repairman the next day, which took three more hot days to arrive.

Finally, I was settled in. My desk was set up under the window and the twin bed was arranged like a day bed with a new cover. My bedroom was an oasis of white and cream. The whole place had a feeling of promise and freedom. Gone was the weight of the condo around my neck. The space vibrated with creative potential. *I could do anything I want.* Maybe I could actually be anything I wanted to be. *Maybe I could be a photographer like I wanted when I was ten or eleven. Maybe I could be a writer like I thought I'd be when I was thirteen.*

I remember sitting in English class, my teacher talking about how writers had influenced the world. I had thought, *Wow! A person can actually change the world through their writing.* I had started to think about what the life of a writer must be like. I didn't like the idea of sitting in one room for hours on end. *And what if I didn't have anything important or interesting to say?* That pretty much ended my desire to be a writer. I couldn't imagine trying to come up with important things to write all the time.

But what about now? The idea of taking a year off to change my life seemed important. *If I could influence other women to reclaim their minds and their power, I really could help improve the world. Maybe I could be a writer. Maybe I should be the one to write the book! Forget all of those ghostwriters. I can do it...can't I?*

Over the next few weeks, I worked on creating a new schedule, incorporating writing, office work and practicing guitar. Over time, working in only one room got to be a bit much, so I experimented with spending time out at cafes writing every other day, as well as different schedules.

One afternoon, I opened up my email to find a message from one of the guys in the kayaking meetup, asking if I wanted to go kayaking sometime. I sat staring at, it not knowing how to respond. On the one hand, I really wanted a kayaking friend. On the other, I didn't want any complications. The experiment was to not date for one year. *Was it not dating if I went kayaking with a guy with the intention of only kayaking?* I decided to put the issue aside for a while and walked away from the computer.

I noticed that the thought of it came back to me over the next couple of hours. The thought of going out with someone new was tantalizing, in the same way a first date is. I could feel my focus getting pulled away. Later, I decided that whatever the intention, it wasn't worth getting distracted or ruining the experiment. *Who am I kidding? I'm not going to be able to just be friends with this guy.* I wrote him back and said that I might be available after October 1st.

Kevin texted me a few minutes later. I was happy to hear from him and texted back, briefly. I wondered if this was cheating on the experiment as well.

He texted back "Why can't you get together until October?"

I replied "Happy to talk about it over the phone. Call me sometime and I'll explain it.

189

He texted back "On my way to class. Will call over the weekend."

That night I printed off a two-year calendar on one sheet and started writing in things I wanted to do over the next year, like the Evaluator's Institute in Atlanta and the Paris Writer's Conference. Maybe I would be a real writer by then. I posted the calendar behind my computer. I installed a budgeting app on my phone to help me adjust to my new income level, and to try to save for some of the trips I was planning. Over the weekend, it occurred to me a couple of times that Kevin was supposed to call, but I never heard from him.

Samantha, a friend from college, posted on Facebook asking if anyone from our Biology Club would be interested in having a reunion in July. I had been looking for an excuse to visit Boston again. The last time I had been there was ten years prior. And when I thought about the experiment and reconnecting with friends, it seemed natural to say yes. Several other members (some of whom I had not even thought of in over fifteen years) responded positively as well. There was much debate over the location, but in the end, Samantha offered to host it in Boston.

***

I am working on getting my new schedule right. I put time on the calendar for meditating, practicing guitar, writing, and doing office work. I am getting things done, but boy, does my schedule feel full! At first, I tried to do writing and office work on the same day for five days a week, but it soon became overwhelming, and I switched it to every other day.

The Bio Club reunion is coming up. I am working on housing accommodations for the trip. Going to Boston seems like a long way for just one party and hotels are expensive in Boston. I need to think of something else to pair the reunion with in order to make the trip worthwhile.

I'm thinking of maybe staying at an ashram. That would solve the housing dilemma and allow me to deepen my spiritual practice. The closest ashram to Boston is an hour away, and intriguingly, it's a Kundalini ashram. Apparently, they have space. Samantha said I could stay at her house on the weekend. I just have to decide about the ashram.

Chapter Thirty-two
Home Away From Home

The morning air was still crisp as I stepped into Koreshan State Park. It felt as if great big arms were reaching out and enfolding me as I walked through the pine trees. My heart swelled and steadied. I smiled. The park was beginning to mean more to me than I had ever imagined a place could. Sunlight filtered through the trees and the scent of pine rose up around me.

My guitar was slung over my shoulder in its soft black case. As I approached the picnic tables along the river, I looked down at my phone and decided to take pictures of the scene in front of me. I thought about my very first camera. My father had let me borrow his boxy, black camera with the leather case when I was eleven years old. I immediately fell in love with the thing. Capturing the perfect image became an obsession. I took so many pictures that my father eventually gave up his claim to the camera, and it became mine.

Now, I didn't even own a camera, except the one built into my phone. It had been a long time since I'd taken a photo that wasn't at a family event or just for the sake of taking a picture. I sat with my back to the picnic table, carefully composing a shot of the live oak on the other bank. Its graceful branches, draped with moss, hung low over the sparkling water. I arranged the shot carefully, using all my knowledge of perspective and balance. Somehow, it still looked flat, like a postcard. I wanted to incorporate the dirt along my side of the bank as well, but no amount of rearranging could change it. It lacked the magical quality of the actual scene.

I was about to give up and was pulling the camera phone away when I happened to glance at the screen as it was descending. *That's the shot*, I thought. I looked at what the lens had been pointing at and took another picture. It wasn't perfectly composed, but it captured the bank of the river and just some of the water and tree. It held the essence of the scene. *That's strange,* I thought. It seemed like the magic wasn't where I thought it would be. Instead, it lay elsewhere, in a place that was somehow in-between.

I decided to try to find that "in-between" place and started clicking pictures. I took a picture of my feet and the dirt. I took a picture of the gentle spots the sun made on the bank, in front of the river. *That is the "real" Koreshan State Park*, I thought. I got up and walked over to the nature trail, snapping pictures of things that caught my eye, eventually reaching the heart vines.

Along the right side of the trail was an area with vines that reached skyward, carrying bright green heart-shaped leaves. I loved this spot. The heart vines always made me happy when I saw them. I snapped pictures of the vines climbing up the trees from afar, and then from close up. I wanted to reproduce the joy of the scene. I smiled and continued my journey up the trail, contemplating joy and magic. *Maybe joy isn't where we think it is... or where we think it should be. Maybe it's in the in-between places, where thought doesn't live.*

***

Journal Entry: 6-15-2012 Women

I've been thinking about the way that so many aspects of our culture lead women to hate themselves. Fashion tells women that if they don't look a certain way, they are worthless. If they don't have a mate, they are worthless. The advertising industry thrives off these feelings of inadequacy. Our whole economy feeds off people thinking they are not enough, so they have to buy more and more and more. Women need to stop hating themselves.

Chapter Thirty-three
A Question of Moths

July

Apparently, Bonita Springs is home to a species of moth that makes cocoons and sticks them all over the exterior of houses, including on the screens on the windows. Of course, my desk was set up right in front of a window. Whenever I looked away from my work, I saw cocoons. I kept saying that I would get a chair and go out to remove them, but I never got around to it. One day, I decided that I couldn't take it anymore. I was standing outside the house looking up at my window (which was much higher than I realized), when I heard a voice behind me. "What are you looking at?"

I turned around to find a good-looking man with short, grayish hair, wearing nothing but a pair of jeans. He had high cheek bones and a chiseled jaw, and was standing on the deck of the house beside ours. He seemed to be holding some kind of tool but I was distracted by his bare, muscular chest.

"I…um…I'm looking at those moths up there. I want to get rid of them," stumbling over my words.

"I'm Christopher," he said with what sounded like a German accent, "Did you just move here?"

"Well, yeah. I'm Geva. I've been here about six weeks, I guess. My desk is right there, and those moth cocoons are in my way," I said, pointing to the window.

He brought a hose over and tried spraying them. Some came off, but not all of them. Next, he brought a ladder over and positioned it next to the window. He climbed up and wiped the cocoons off with a cloth.

"Thanks," I said, trying not to notice his chiseled abdomen.

"No problem. If you need anything, just come by."

I excused myself and walked away thinking, *Okay, that's not good. A hot looking 40 year old lives next door to me... damn*!

A few days later, I arrived home at the same time as him. I was getting my mail from the mailbox just as he stepped out of his pick-up truck.

He greeted me, and we chatted for a few minutes.

"How is everything?" he asked.

"Good. Everything's fine," I replied. "Is that a kayak on your back deck?" I tried to sound casual, but I was already regretting the question.

"Yes, I sometimes take it out near Lover's Key. But I really don't know anybody around here. If you ever want to do anything, just let me know," he said.

"Um, okay," I said walking away.

Over the next week, I was too busy packing for my trip to think about much else. And yet, the thought of my hot-looking neighbor next door kept intruding on my thoughts. *Could it hurt to hang out with him occasionally? Maybe it could be perfectly harmless, just hanging out and doing things together…*

***

By Friday, I was ready for some fun. As I drove along, it occurred to me that my anxiety level was fairly low, considering that I was going to a place where I would know hardly anyone. I was headed to a "Live Art" event that my guitar instructor's band was playing at. There was supposed to be a drum circle, and he had invited me to join in. I was having trouble finding the event. The address I'd been given placed me at a nondescript strip mall in southern Naples. The sun was setting, and there were some people milling around in front of one of the units, but it was the wrong address. Further to the left, there were two people standing at an open door. One of them was dressed all in black. "That must be it," I thought.

The "Live Art" event was supposed to have community art-making to live music, with everybody adding their piece to a communal art project. When I reached the door, a smug-looking guy with short black hair and black pants asked me to park at the next building. I handed him my drum and went back to move my car. Upon entering the dimly-lit room, I could see large, colorful paintings on the dark walls. To my left, was a stage area and there were several tables scattered about. I said hello to a few people and the owner who showed me around.

Kirk was setting up his musical gear, but took a break to greet me.

197

"Hey, Geva. Nice to see you, honey," he said, hugging me.

"Hi Kirk. Where will the drum circle be?"

"The drummers will be on stage with the band," he said, motioning to the other side of the room.

"I'm going to finish setting up now. Just make yourself at home," he told me with a smile.

There were little groups of people here and there, but no one seemed to be very friendly. They all seemed to be in their own little worlds. Nobody even said "hello" to me as I walked around. There was a big, vertical sign hanging on the wall that looked like graffiti on the side of a subway car. It said "Live Art," and at the bottom was a small Buddha statue with glowing candles. The lighting looked so beautiful that I took a picture, then walked around a bit, capturing more images. *I wonder where the other drummers are...*

Just then, Kirk came up and said, "Show Time!" He guided me toward the stage.

"Oh...okay....where are the other drummers?" I stammered looking around.

"I guess they didn't show up," he said, guiding me onto the stage. "No problem. You will be sitting here behind the lead singer," he said, pointing out the spot and moving a stool into place.

The reality that there were no other drummers, and that I would be playing alone with the band *ON STAGE* was hitting me. Perspiration broke out under my arms. The singer came onstage. She was about 25, with long, black hair and tight miniskirt. She studiously avoided me. "Geva, this is Jessica. Geva will be joining us for the evening."

"Oh, hi," she said, turning back to adjust her microphone.

I settled into place with the drum between my knees. A school performance flashed through my mind. I was waiting for the long, heavy curtains to open so I could say my two lines. I was so nervous that I almost peed my pants. A guy named Mike was holding the ropes to the curtains, and tried to calm me down by making jokes. It was to no avail because when the curtains finally opened, my mind went blank. Someone prompted me from off-stage, and I stammered through my two lines before fleeing for safety backstage.

But, this didn't feel quite as bad. Kirk had chosen a variety of 60s songs. The songs were fun and it wasn't too hard to fly under the radar. The band was so loud that it was pretty hard to hear my un-miked drum anyway. I was focused on finding a rhythm and trying not to look like a fool. I pretty much followed the actual drummer.

Hey, this is kind of fun, I thought. *Somewhat surreal, but kind of fun.* And I was fulfilling a lifelong dream to play with a band. *Of course, I had always pictured myself singing with a band, not necessarily playing a djembe, but I was still playing with a band.* And Kirk and the guys were really nice to me. There was a break at 10:00 pm. We all took pictures and then I headed out into the night.

***

Journal Entry: 6-2-2012

I saw an amazing video last night. An anthropologist named Helen Fisher gave a TED talk called "The Brain in Love." She discussed her research investigating why humans crave love so much. She and her research team had taken MRIs of people in love, and of people who had just been dumped. They then analyzed the data and found that there is a distinct similarity between the brain in love and the brain on major drugs like cocaine. Really interesting....

Chapter Thirty-four
Mom

That Sunday, my mother and I drove to the drum circle together. If she hadn't been willing to go, I probably would have skipped it, as I was still tired from the night before. The highway was closed, so we met up at the CVS and then we drove North on a local road. As we drove, smoke from a brush fire wafted through the air as storm clouds gathered.

This was the first chance we had to talk in a while and I wanted to use our time wisely, to talk about meaningful things.

"Mom, I've been learning a lot from this experiment."

"Really? Like what?" she asked, curiously. "I didn't know you were still doing that."

"Yes, the experiment is for a whole year, Mom. Anyway, one of the most important things seems to be about building reserves," I said

"What do you mean "reserves?" Like savings?" she rolled up the window.

"Kind of, but not just money. Reserves can be anything. Basically, you work on filling up whatever you need and then building a surplus."

"So, what kind of reserves have you been building?" she looked confused.

"Well, I started with the basics, like buying all of my dry goods a year in advance. But now, I'm trying to build a reserve of energy and time..." I said trying to think of examples.

"I think I understand," she said.

"Mom, I worry about you. You work so hard and you give out all of your energy to everyone else. You hardly have any time for yourself," I said, gripping the steering wheel.

"Well, that's true," she said wistfully.

I asked her when was the last time she had taken a day for herself.

"Well, I... I can't remember. Maybe a few weeks ago..."

"And you keep getting sick. It's like you have no reserve of energy. You spend your energy like a drunken sailor," I said, trying to stay calm despite my concern.

"Yes, I never looked at it that way."

"Couldn't you set aside at least one day that was just for you?" She smiled but there was a weariness in her eyes.

"I'll try honey. At least we have today."

"Yes, at least we have today, Mom." Drum circles were nothing new to my mother, being a hippie from way back. For some reason, she preferred to dance at the circles instead of drum. Dancing always brought her such joy. I was glad she would have the chance tonight.

As we drove on, the rain began, but by the time we arrived, the sky was clear. The sound of drumming greeted us as we reached the park. I dropped my mother at the entrance to the gazebo, and went to park. I lugged in my heavy drum, some friendly faces called out "Hello!" "Geva!!!!" Donna called out. She had a radiant smile on her face. I went over to her and held out my hand. "Hi honey," I said, dropping a big, pink sparkly flower pendant on a long chain into her hand.

"I love it!" she exclaimed. Donna had admired my necklace one day. Later, I saw the same one on sale at my favorite jewelry store, so I picked one up for her. I had only known her for a few months from coming to the drum circle, but she seemed to be one of the happiest, nicest people around. I wanted to repay some of the joy she gave out so freely.

I set up my drum in front of a picnic table. Some people were already drumming. Mary was there, in her colorful sarong and feather earrings. Stuart was behind the bongos and a there were a few djembe players. My mother was milling around, saying hello to everyone. She looked so happy.

I ignored the blond woman who sat to my left and she ignored me as usual. She had always seemed strange. She had ignored me the first two or three drum circles I had visited and then said some slightly rude things when we were finally introduced. She seemed like the kind of woman who was extremely threatened by other women, whom she thought might try to steal her man. I had no interest in her boyfriend, but she never seemed to notice that. I thought it best to ignore her.

Someone started a good rhythm and I began drumming. Donna looked over and I held up my pendant. She held up hers in response and smiled broadly. Next to Donna were two older ladies with drums. Their husbands sat behind them at a picnic table. I enjoyed following the rhythm. My drumming was improving little by little.

In between rhythms the blond woman turned and said, "Sooooo, Geeeva, how are you?"

"Good thanks. How are you?"

She looked at me pointedly. "You don't remember my name do you?"

"No, I don't," I said, and kept drumming.

Mary came into the circle with two little girls who had brightly colored scarves, fringed with gold coins. They looked like miniature belly dancers. Mary prompted them to dance. I couldn't tell if they were related to Mary or not. The younger one had a short, blond bob, and looked like a deer in headlights. The older girl moved her hips back and forth in awkward shapes. Everyone smiled at them and kept on drumming.

My mother came in and danced with the girls, delight radiating from her face as she twirled around.

I turned to the blond woman and said, "Sandy, right?"

"You did remember!" she exclaimed.

"It just came to me," I said, and kept drumming. *I might as well be polite,* I thought. People moved in and out of the circle, and some new drummers joined. A very dark-skinned teenaged boy in a black top hat joined in, drumming at a table behind me. George arrived, to cheers from the group. The drumming went on building in waves, waxing and waning.

Before I knew it, it was getting late and we had to get on the road. On the way home the highway was open and we whizzed along. "That was so much fun," My Mom said.

"Yes, it was. I'm really glad you could make it," I told her.

***

The night before my flight to Boston, I decided to stop by to see my neighbor. I didn't want to leave for the trip without finding out a little more about him. *Who is this guy? What is he like? Am I going to wonder about him the entire time I'm gone?* I went over and knocked on his front door. There was no answer. As I turned to leave, the door suddenly swung open. "Hi there, come on in," Christopher said with a grin.

His place was clean and sparse.

"Nice place," I said, impressed with the neatness.

"Thanks, I like modern style, don't you?" As a matter of fact, I found it hideous. But, I tried to think of something polite to say.

"Well, it's lovely."

"Thanks. Would you like a glass of wine?" He had some sort of smarmy look on his face, as if this was some kind of seduction scene. I felt slightly nauseated.

"Oh, no thanks," I said, backing away. "I don't drink. I really should be going. I just wanted to stop by and say hello," I said, making my way to the door.

"Uh, okay. Well, I'll see you later," he said, as I made my way out.

Chapter Thirty-five
Boston

I was on a shuttle to the airport when the call came in. Four strangers and the shuttle driver glanced over at the loudly ringing phone in my hand. I looked around, feeling a little uncomfortable taking a call in public. *Maybe I should let it go to voice mail,* I thought. I decided to take a chance and answered it.

"Hi, I'm looking for Geva Salerno," a voice said.

"This is Geva. What can I do for you?"

"Geva, my name is Karen. I'm with the Naples Symphony Orchestra. You were referred to me by Penny Robertson and a few people on my board of directors. We're looking for someone to help us with some strategic planning," she said. "Did I get you at a bad time?"

I knew the organization. They had a long history in the area, and had recently undergone some leadership changes. "I would be happy to help you. In fact, I specialize in strategic planning," I told her. "But, at the moment, I'm about to get on a plane, heading out of town. Could I bother you to email me with the information?"

"Oh, absolutely, and I'm so happy you're interested," she said. We exchanged contact information and hung up. I sat back in the van and marveled at my luck. The Naples Symphony Orchestra was one of the largest and most prestigious organizations in the area. *This seems like a good sign.*

I hadn't been back to Boston in over ten years, and although I'd moved around a lot, I still considered it home. Sitting on the plane, I wondered how it would be to see my old stomping grounds again. *Would it be the same? Would I fit back in? How would I feel, being back there again?*

After disembarking and collecting my rental car, I headed out into the Boston traffic. The buildings looked the same, but something felt different. I couldn't quite place it. I had spent ten years in Florida, the first eight feeling marooned and missing Boston. During the last two years, however, I had come to an acceptance of the fact that I had chosen Florida for a reason. My family was there and wherever they were is where I wanted to be. But part of me still yearned for the excitement and intellectual stimulation of Boston. I missed the feeling that anything was possible. *Anything is possible in Boston...*

I tried to navigate using the maps I had printed, but ended up getting lost twice. *Okay, remain calm,* I thought, and took a deep breath. Eventually, I found my way out to the countryside and the road to the ashram. In the late afternoon light, the sight of the colonial homes grabbed my heart. I had forgotten how charming country towns in Massachusetts can be.

I wasn't prepared for the wave of nostalgia that poured over me. The solidly built two-story houses made me think of the permanence that didn't exist in my life. These homes had been around for hundreds of years. They were part of a community that didn't change. The people in these homes stayed in one place, and grew and flourished...

together. *I used to live in towns with houses like this,* I thought. *I used to be a part of this.* A number of houses had red, metal stars on their fronts. I later found out that it was the town's three hundredth birthday that year and the stars were a part of the celebration.

Driving along the windy country road, I almost passed the ashram. The long driveway bordered an enormous lawn surrounded by pasture fencing. Two three-story buildings faced the road. I drove by a few people dressed in white. Some wore turbans of one sort or another. After inquiring about the guest quarters, a guy in his late twenties dragged my suitcase up three flights of stairs. Another woman, also dressed in white showed me around the apartment, leaving me to choose a bedroom.

No one was around. The sparsely decorated quarters had three bedrooms on each floor. I chose the most private one, with a mattress on the floor, a chair, and a fan. On the first morning I didn't know what to do. Unlike Kripalu, this ashram had no agenda. Just resting and relaxing didn't seem like a good use of my time. A tall girl with short, brown hair dressed in white shorts and a tee shirt came into the kitchen. "Hi," I said happy to have company.

"Hi, there. Are you here for the workshop?" She had a German accent.

"No, I'm just here for a few days, to relax I guess. My name's Geva," I said.

"I'm Neela," she replied.

"How long have you been here?" I opened some hot cereal I had brought.

"Almost two months now. Tomorrow's my last day," she said looking forlorn.

"Oh. How did you spend your time here?" I asked.

"Mostly doing yoga and helping in the garden," she said with a smile.

"Wow! That sounds cool," I said. I hadn't worked in a garden in years. "Do you think I could work in the garden?" I was hopeful, thinking of the sun and dirt.

After a few phone calls, I was out in a huge, thoroughly overgrown garden with Jaynie the garden manager. Jaynie wore a flowing, gray cotton dress and long gloves. Her thick, brown hair was twisted into a braid that rested on one shoulder. She had recently returned from two months abroad, and the garden had gotten out of control in her absence. I helped her in weeding the three rows of five-foot beds, surrounded by long ditches. Jaynie was content with pulling weeds by hand, but that method left a lot behind and didn't remove the roots. I couldn't stand the thought of the weeds growing back quickly.

I found a shovel and set about digging up two beds. It was a clear, sunny day. A cool breeze kept us company as we silently went about our tasks. After finishing the weeding, I found a wheel-barrow and removed several loads of weeds that we had pulled out. After two hours, I was sweaty, sore, and covered with dirt. Jaynie seemed surprised when I excused myself. Suddenly, relaxing sounded like a good thing to me.

After cleaning up, I went into town for food. In addition to enough food to last several days, I bought some cupcakes to celebrate Neela's last night. Although I hardly knew her, I knew what it was like to finish something really meaningful and need closure. On the drive back, I started to feel the effects of my hard work weeding in the garden. I knew that it would be an early night.

Back at the guest quarters, I presented the cupcakes to Neela.

"That is so nice of you!" she seemed happy. "I really appreciate it."

We sat in the kitchen eating our cupcakes and she told me about her life in Germany. I asked her about German men, remembering my hot-looking neighbor back home. Her comments about German men taking their time in relationships were encouraging, but their lack of subtlety combined with their inability to even comprehend it, did not seem attractive.

That night I decided to take a Kundalini yoga class. Having no idea what to expect, I walked in and found only one other person, sitting on a mat to my left. I wondered if there would be anyone else joining us. At the front of the room, sitting on a bench up on a platform was a gentleman, wearing a white tunic and pants. The man had a long, dark beard and piercing black eyes, which found me as I took a mat. He reminded me of the Sikhs of Northern India who wear elaborate turbans and carry tremendous swords.

"Hello, welcome," he said. "Please find a spot." He motioned to the right of the other man.

"What is your background with Kundalini yoga?" he inquired. I felt like a little like an intruder, but I was ready.

"Pretty much none."

"You'll do fine," he said. We waited a few more minutes, but no one arrived. The instructor explained that each class focused on one kriya. Apparently, each kriya is intended to achieve a specific result with the ultimate aim of awakening the Kundalini energy and guiding it up the spine to reach enlightenment, or bliss.

I didn't realize that each class would be dedicated to something specific. This was completely unlike hatha yoga classes, which while great for relaxation and stretching, were somewhat random in what they covered. That night's kriya was designed to open the meridians of the front of the body, specifically along the arms and legs.

The class was like no other class I had ever taken. The instructor followed instructions from a text, reading aloud as we went along. We did a lot of short, rapid movements with our arms and legs. Luckily, I had strengthened my core with Hatha yoga, because a lot of Kundalini seemed to involve lying on my back, raising my legs up and down, and coordinating the movement with my breath. It was quite challenging. At one point I wasn't sure if I was going to make it. My classmate and I struggled to follow the instructions. When I looked over, his face was red and sweat was pouring off his forehead.

By the time we finished, my t-shirt was drenched and I could feel a bead of sweat run down between my shoulder blades.

"Okay, lie down in stillness," the instructor said. He made his way over to a big gong on the other side of the room. As we lay there the sound of the gong shimmered, building in strength and waning alternately like a bath of sound rolling over and encompassing us. My mind became one with the sound. All thought vanished and only the sound existed. Eventually, the gong subsided. We slowly sat up.

Then there was a closing meditation in which we held our arms up at shoulder level and moved our fingers in

212

concentric circles while repeating a mantra. This went on for quite a while, and I began to mix up the words. Eventually, the instructor told us to stop, and we sat in silence. After a few moments, we opened our eyes and the instructor closed the book.

"You are strong," he said, looking at me.

"Oh. Um, thanks," I said. I was taken off guard. My rosy cheeks blushed a deeper shade of pink. His comment meant a lot to me, coming from a Kundalini instructor who could probably slice me in half with a sword.

The next day I drove to Samantha's house, using the GPS program I had downloaded onto my phone. I was determined not to get lost, not to have a stressful experience. Because I had some extra time, I drove to our alma mater first, which was practically up the street from her house. UMass sits on a peninsula and as I drove up, I recalled of all the sunny days I had spent there.

Since it was the middle of the summer, the campus was empty. When I walked into the Student Union Building, I didn't recognize a thing, except for a familiar face coming up the stairs. "Hello professor," I said, knowing he didn't recognize me.

"Heading home, finally," He said, and passed with a slightly quizzical look. "Doc" Hagar was one of the principal biology professors at UMass Boston. Since he'd taught thousands of students over the years, it didn't surprise me that he didn't recognize me. I thought of the time I had pulled up my shirt to expose my new belly-button ring to my fellow lab students.

"What is that?!" he had exclaimed, shock and amusement on his face. I chuckled at the memory, and kept walking. The biochemistry students had been an odd lot, very quiet and studious for the most part. *The biology students were the wild and crazy ones.*

The buildings were still connected by a glass catwalk, and I made my way from one to the next looking for something... *What am I looking for?* I thought. *Clues to my past? Pieces of my past?* I found the science building, but it appeared that the Biology Club no longer existed. *Time has moved on without me.* There were so many new building. I found the top of the circular stairway where I had stood with a boyfriend one day between exams. I remember that I was eating French fries and trying not to worry about finals. His presence had calmed me. *So much fear back then*, I thought.

Those halls were literally drenched with my stress for four years. Okay, five. I didn't graduate on time. Something in me insisted on getting a degree that I (and the world) would respect. My first choice would have been physics, not because I particularly liked physics, but because it seemed like the hardest possible degree ever. When it comes to respect, really who gets more than a physicist? But, that had not even seemed even remotely possible. So, I tried chemistry.

The first semester was difficult. The second was even more difficult. I had been standing outside one of the professor's office, waiting, when I happened to notice a piece of paper taped to the door with the requirements for the biochemistry degree. *Hmm, that looks easier*, I had thought, *and interesting too.* I inquired about it and switched immediately.

I ended up having some really thought-provoking classes. I enjoyed all of the theory, but I especially loved learning about the systems within the human body and nature. One class, physical chemistry, had me on the edge of my seat. It was known as the hardest class one could possibly take, but I loved it. The combination of physics, chemistry, and calculus was like mental gymnastics. We had learned each subject separately in previous courses, but here we got to actually use them simultaneously! Most of the other students seemed to be falling asleep and were somewhat mystified as to why I asked so many questions and was so enthusiastic. I was riveted.

But when it came to the labs, I was lost. My poor study habits really showed. I would consistently show up to the labs unprepared, having failed to read the lab material ahead of time. I never knew what was going on, and hated every minute of it. Thinking back to those labs made me glad I had completed that chapter of my life. I left the campus and headed out to find Samantha's house.

After parking in front of the row of townhouses, I somehow managed to walk straight up to the wrong door and ring the bell.

"Can I help you?" a man said, opening the door.

"I'm looking for Samantha," I said.

"There's no Samantha here."

"Uh, okay," I said. Samantha's house was two doors down.

The same Samantha I had known 15 years before showed me into the three-story house she and her boyfriend, Declan were renovating. There were boards and sheet rock in the hallway and bags of plaster in the living room. Samantha introduced me to her four year old son, Pierce, and gave me a tour. Physically, she looked the same. She had always been thin. Even after gaining some weight, she still looked skinny.

Reconnecting with her felt good, like I was adding back a piece of my self that I had left behind or misplaced on my journey. We talked about the twists and turns our lives had taken. Samantha was still one of the most interesting people I had ever met. She had been fourteen when she entered UMass. She had faked the date on her application, and no one had ever found out. She didn't look her age, so none of us had thought anything of it. When it all eventually came out, I was bewildered. I had sisters just a few years younger than her and I had to fight the urge to treat her like one of them.

Samantha excelled at science, but she was also an accomplished dancer. I took my sisters to see her perform in the Nutcracker a few times back then. At one point she wasn't sure whether to pursue science or dance. She eventually ended up getting a dual degree in math and biology.

"I always wondered whether you would become a scientist or a dancer," I said. We were sitting at the tall, table in her kitchen.

"Well, I spent a few years partying and trying to figure my life out after college. That's how I met Declan, at a pub. Those were the partying days."

"I totally get that, Samantha. I mean, I can see how it would take a little while to make sense of all that. You were so young when you were in school."

"Yes, it didn't make sense for a while. It was my dad's idea that I go to UMass because the public high schools were so bad where we lived. I didn't really think of myself as a genius or anything."

"Well, you did get like straight A's. Anyway, what did you do after that?"

"I did a little teaching and then went back for my master's degree. I liked teaching, but I needed to make some money. So, now teaching is part of my job. I train people on scientific instruments."

"Cool," I said imagining her in a lab explaining how a new piece of equipment worked.

"You know, not that many of us are actually working in science now," she said.

"Yes, I've gathered that from what I've seen on Facebook," I replied.

"I've been thinking that there should really be some kind of interim step before graduating, like an internship program or something," she said, leaning forward over the table.

"You know, that's a great idea. You should tell Doc that. I saw him at UMass just now. He looks exactly the same," I said.

"Yes, I see him all the time. Anyway, what about you? What have you been up to? You went to India after college, right?"

I described the twists and turns my life had taken and eventually got to the part about the experiment.

"That sounds really cool," she said. "How has it been going?"

"Really good," I replied. "I feel like I can finally breathe. My whole world is changing." I described a few of the changes I had made so far.

"Wow, that's awesome," she said. I appreciated her support. We went on to discuss our mutual friends and how their lives had turned out.

That evening, the four of us ate dinner together. Despite a 15 year age difference, Samantha and Declan seemed pretty happy. They couldn't be more different. Declan was straight from Ireland and worked as a carpenter and she had grown up south of Boston and worked for a pharmaceutical company. But there was an easy affection between them. It was funny to see Samantha interact with Pierce. She seemed somewhat mystified by him, always wondering what he was going to say next.

The next day I took the subway into Boston proper to continue my journey down memory lane. I got off at the Downtown Crossing stop and emerged into a crowd of people bustling about. I walked up Summer Street to the intersection of Tremont, stopping to take a picture of a piece of artwork hanging suspended between two buildings. It was made up of hundreds of shiny little discs that shimmered as they moved in the breeze. *What purpose did the piece serve? It wasn't advertising anything, and yet it was in a public space. It must be art.*

I walked down Tremont past the Commons and crossed over to Boylston Street. Walking along the park, I noticed some ancient gravestones with intricate carvings. I stopped to take some more pictures. Up ahead, there were ducks playing at the edge of a pond. Beyond them a man was entertaining a small group of people with a multitude of instruments strapped to his body, *truly a one man band*, I thought. Further up Boylston, I passed the building I had worked in for several years before college as a barber. I didn't go inside, but captured the image and moved on. The owner at the tiny barber shop had died of a brain tumor, and I didn't care to see if the shop was even there anymore.

I took Berkeley over to Newbury, curious to see the glitzy shops and trendy fashions. At the intersection, a young guy had set up a table with clothing and jewelry. His products had an edgy, street quality to them. When I asked about his work, he told me that the main design "We Run Bos" had a double meaning. It was for runners, but it also suggested that the people are really the ones who run Boston. He gave me a card directing me to his website. The card was very well-designed and it was interesting the way he combined high and low tech. His shop, it seemed, had no overhead. Something about his work intrigued me...

I continued on my journey, hoping to see some more edgy, cool stuff near the top of Newbury Street. All the creative stuff used to be there. But, passing by the shops there didn't seem to be much going on anymore. *What exactly am I looking for?* I thought. I didn't want to buy anything. I just wanted, *what?*

I was getting hungry, so I got on the subway and headed for Harvard Square.

I had worked in Harvard Square cutting hair in the oldest barber shop in Boston, just prior to entering college full time. La Flamme was owned by a Greek man named George, who had been in his late 50's at the time. He had thick gray hair that he wore combed straight back. *I wonder who owns the shop now*, I thought as I walked up the sidewalk. When I looked in the window, I was shocked to see George at the first chair, just finishing with a customer.

The shop looked exactly the way I remembered it. It was packed with customers, every one of the eight chairs filled. There was still the striking mahogany furniture and crystal chandeliers overhead. The opulence was always a contrast to the plain, navy-blue, short sleeved jackets we wore. We looked like mechanics, but our dress somehow underscored the down to earth atmosphere and focus on quality. I walked in and stood next to George's chair. Clearly, he didn't recognize me.

"Hi George," I said, when he glanced over.

"Hi," He said turning to take the fee from his client. "Hey, I know you! Geva, from Cape Cod, right?" His Greek accent was as thick as I remembered. I smiled.

"How've you been?" he asked smiling.

"Good. I live in Florida now. How's everything here?"

"Good. Good," he said looking around at the line of customers waiting.

"Well, I'll let you go. I just wanted to say hello," I said, taking my leave.

"It was nice to see you. Take care of yourself," he said, as he guided another customer to the chair.

"Thanks." *Only an experienced barber would appreciate the brevity of a conversation like that,* I thought. I turned and made my way through the people milling around.

Harvard Square hadn't changed much. There were lots of new stores, but still the same youthful, hip vibe. The diversity and number of young people struck me. After living in Florida for so long, the presence of so many people under the age of fifty was a bit jarring and refreshing. But there was something else. *Something else is different...* As I made my way through the brick buildings across the square to Brattle Street, I wondered if Evan would be at George's other shop. Evan was George's nephew, and my age. Although he had managed the shop for George for years, he also had an entrepreneurial side to him. Before we met, he had run his own record store for several years. He had probably left years ago, and must now be in a new job, with a new life, probably even in a new state.

Evan and I were friends for quite some time. I always appreciated his terrific sense of humor and his sweet soul. He and his sister had taken care of his mother for years when she was dying. He never complained or wished for anything different. He just did what he had to do. We used to sit in the shop and talk for hours. We tried dating once or twice but it didn't feel quite right. Nevertheless, we had stayed friends. I assumed that after his mother died he had started a whole new life.

I looked in the shop window. There was Evan, working on a customer. I couldn't believe it. The small shop was long and narrow, with barely enough room for four barbers and their clients. I came in and stood by the door but Evan clearly didn't recognize me. "Can I help you?" he asked. When I smiled, his face lit up. "Geva. Oh my goodness! Come on in... Can you wait a few minutes?" I looked at the guy in the chair and the other one waiting.

"Sure, but I could come back in a bit. Why don't I walk around and come back?"

"Sure! It's so great to see you! I'll be free in about 20 minutes," he said, looking at the clock.

I walked around Harvard Square visiting a few shops and browsing. When I went back, Evan was just finishing up. We sat down in the two front waiting chairs, facing each other. We talked about our lives and what had happened since we had last seen each other. "I've been helping a friend of mine. She's sick... She's really sick," he said, looking away.

"What do you mean?" I asked.

"She has all kinds of problems. I go over her house after work and bring her groceries. Stuff like that."

"Is this a girlfriend, Evan?"

"Well, we kind of dated a while ago, but..."

"I understand," I said trying not to look surprised.

"She can barely walk, Geva."

"Wow, that's really awful," I said, looking out the window.

I didn't know what to think. On the one hand he was doing something noble and selfless, but on the other I was sad to hear that he was stuck in this situation again. His life consisted of taking care of someone else's every need. When would he get to enjoy himself, express himself?

"So, what brings you to town?" he asked.

"I'm here for a reunion. But, I wanted to stop by and say hello..."

"That's great. I'm so glad you did. It's so good to see you.""

"Evan, I'm at a point in my life where I'm recognizing the importance of friends."

He took my hands in his and said "Geva, this is what it's all about. We get to a certain point and we realize that material possessions mean nothing. Nothing. It's about friends, and family, and moments, and nothing more." I was touched that he felt that way, and that we could have such a real, authentic conversation after so much time. "I'm so glad you came to visit."

"I am too, Evan. I'm glad you're doing well," I said. We hugged goodbye and I headed out to Samantha's house.

The next day, Samantha and I left early to buy supplies for the reunion.

"I wonder if anyone will even show up," she said. Only one person had made a positive RSVP.

"Well, I think we should prepare for a fair number, just in case. Don't you?"

"Yes, let's prepare for a dozen people and hope for the best," she said. We bought enough soda and snacks for twelve. On the ride over, I wondered what my classmates were up to nowadays. *Were they all fabulously successful? How would my life compare to theirs? Should I even care?*

When we arrived at the park Samantha had chosen for the reunion, there was no one there. Declan took Pierce to play at the playground, and Samantha and I spread the table cloth out on a picnic table and set out the snacks. By 1:00 pm, the appointed time, no one had shown up.

We were starting to get worried when Andrew and his two daughters arrived. Andrew and I had never been close, but it was still nice to see him. He had always seemed kind of arrogant and elitist with his preppy clothes and smug attitude.

"What are you doing nowadays, Andrew?" Samantha asked.

"I'm in staffing for a pharmaceutical company," he said. I wondered how that compared with the plans he had made.

"I work for Big Pharma too," Samantha said. "I train people on using the equipment."

Karen, who had consistently strived for perfect grades, arrived a few minutes later. She looked exactly the same with a big smile, long black hair and clear, tan skin. We were all catching up when Doc and a few others showed up.

I don't think Doc realized that we had passed each other in the hall just a few days prior. Leaning back on his heels, he explained that he was now associate dean of Biology at UMass.

"Part of my job is to interface with biology student alumni," he said. "What have you all been up to?" He seemed to be surprised to hear that so many of us did not go into science or medicine.

Karen said "Well, I did research for a while, but that didn't work out. Now, I'm a Pilates instructor," she said smiling. *What?* That did not compute. *One of the smartest girls in our class was a Pilates instructor?* She said that she enjoyed it, but I couldn't tell if she really meant it.

I had always looked up to Doc, feeling like I would never earn his respect because my poor grades. Now, he was looking at me expectantly. "I have a small consulting firm," I said. "We specialize in management consulting for nonprofits." I found it immensely interesting that I couldn't care less what he thought of my career choice now.

Doc looked a little surprised that none of us were actual scientists.

"Doc, I think that UMass needs to do better with preparing people to get jobs in the industry," Samantha said.

"Hmmm. You might have something there," he replied, looking thoughtful.

"There should be some kind of internship program for science students," she continued. I smiled. I was glad she had gotten the nerve up to tell him. They continued the discussion off to the side.

As I looked at all of them, I felt completely content with the choices I had made. *I like my life,* I thought. *And I'm happy with the choices I made.*

Chapter Thirty-six
Home Again

Back in Naples, I tried to make sense of everything that had taken place on the Boston trip. In some ways, Boston seemed exactly the same. George and Evan were still in Harvard Square. Samantha was still connected to Boston and the Biology Club, and yet something was different. It didn't feel the same.

A piece of my heart had been in Boston for the past 10 years. I knew that. Whenever anyone would talk about how wonderful the weather was in Florida, I would think - *So what?! It's not Boston.* Boston had represented fun, excitement and intellectual stimulation. I could do anything and be anything in Boston. What I didn't realize was how much the fantasy of Boston had been getting in the way of creating a fully satisfying life.

I had always thought about returning someday, but I wanted to be near my family. I wanted to see my nieces and nephews grow up. I wanted to really know my sisters, not just catch up with occasional phone calls. And I wanted to spend time with my parents as they got older. I wanted to be part of something, not just alone adrift in a big, cold city. So I had tucked the Boston-shaped piece of my heart away and refused to look at it, shoving it further down, while I tried to live in Florida. But while I went about living my life in Florida, part of me was on auto-pilot. I could never fully commit to being there.

It seemed that while I roamed the streets of Boston and Harvard Square, I was looking for that missing piece. But in reality what I really wanted didn't exist in Boston anymore. Boston just didn't call to me anymore. UMass was just a building. The subway was no longer a conduit to all places potential, it was just a subway. Yes, Boston was bustling and alive, but I had already proven myself. There was nothing more I wanted to do there.

And so, finally, that small part of my heart was back where it belonged (inside my chest) and I was one step closer to being fully present in my own life. I was also one step closer to being able fully present with the people who mattered to me most, my family and friends.

***

I had arranged for Jeanie, Starbo and George to come over to practice drumming. I was excited and a little nervous. Not only would this be the first time they were coming over, it would be the first time I had guests in the new house. Pam was in the Naples house, so she wouldn't be around. "Do you guys want to practice out on the back porch?" I asked as they entered.

"I don't know, it's a little humid out there," Jeanie said. I had baked brownies and had hummus and chips for everyone and arranged them out on the counter. I had always assumed that whenever you invited people to your home, you should provide food, but no one seemed hungry. They just wanted to drum.

"Well, we could practice in here," I said, motioning to the living room. I nervously gulped down one brownie after the other. *Damn, these brownies are good,* I thought, partially because these were rare gluten-free brownies and partly from nerves.

"Let's start with some drills," Jeanie said. We patted the drums in rhythmic movements, focusing on accentuating the difference between the base, tap, and slap sounds. The base sound was made by gently hitting the center of the drum. The tap and slaps sounds were made by hitting the edge of the drum either with fingers together or spread apart. Base, base, tap, tap, slap, slap. Base, base, tap, tap, slap, slap. I tried to focus on the movements, but I kept thinking: *you're going to mess up. you're going to mess up and then you will be off-beat and everyone will notice. Shut up mind.* **Base base, tap, tap, slap, slap...**

We played some easy rhythms and then Jeanie taught us one and we followed her lead. It was touch and go, because we had never practiced together before. *I'm actually keeping up*, I thought happily. It wasn't clear who, if anyone, was leading the group. I was glad to be part of something like that. Each of us was contributing to something that we were creating together. We played for a few hours and I felt pretty satisfied with our work.

We decided to meet again the following Tuesday at Riverside Park, around the corner from my place. Luckily for me it was halfway between Fort Myers, where Jeanie and Starbo lived, and Naples, where George lived. When I arrived, George was already set up with his chair and drum on the empty stage. The openness of the bandshell felt intimidating.

I set my chair up with its back to the wall, facing out on the lawn. "Where are Jeanie and Starbo?" I asked George.

"You know them. Time is kind of fluid with Jeanie." Jeanie and Starbo arrived 20 minutes later, saying something about being held up. We set the stools up facing together in a small circle. This time, I had a hard time focusing on the drumming. Not only was the openness of the space distracting, but I was acutely aware of the difference in our abilities. Jeanie and Starbo had been drumming for a year and a half and I had only been drumming a few months. Apparently, George had decades of practice.

I had to stop a few times to re-orient myself. George frowned, saying "If you get lost, stop, but come back in. If you just stop it throws the whole thing off," I gritted my teeth in embarrassment. But, we managed to get a few good rhythms going. Jeanie and Starbo started rhythms and we all tried to stay on the same beat. The deep base of the drums sounded good in the air. Afterward, we celebrated by going to the Mexican restaurant around the corner and over dinner, shared some stories and laughs. An easy camaraderie emerged.

Later that week, I asked George to come over and help me with my guitar playing. I knew it was risky because it could have been misinterpreted. I knew that he knew very clearly that I was in the middle of a year-long experiment, but I wanted to improve my guitar playing, and I also wanted to hang out with him. He seemed so laid back and cool. I just wanted to be around him. The 28 Laws of Attraction say to ask people for their time if you want it. So, I did. *Practicing guitar doesn't count as dating, does it?*

229

"Hey, how's it going?" he said, when I opened the door. We set up in the living room. Once again, the porch was too hot. We got the guitars out and spread the pages of music around, so that we could go over what I had been learning.

"I don't know. 'Sweet Home Alabama' seems a little advanced for a beginner," he said looking doubtful. "Let's do this. Why don't you slow down a bit and work on perfecting some of the chords you already know." He patiently strummed along as I worked on perfecting my technique. I focused on making each sound of the chords come out clearly, adjusting my fingers until the sounds were clear.

He didn't seem to be in any hurry to get anywhere with the practice. There was no time limit, just the music. Something about that made me start to choke up. This was the first time I had just sat with someone, with no agenda, and no time limit in as long as I could remember. I tried to blink back the tears. I was trying to focus on the playing, but I was also remembering about how with Bryan we were always racing from one activity to another with a perfectly choreographed schedule. The only time I had his complete attention was in bed, and then it was off to something else.

"So, you said you're retired. What's that like?" I asked.

"Oh, it's great. I have plenty of time to play music and I spend a lot of time outside. I love it," he said strumming. "What about you? I take it you're still working?"

"Yes, I'm still working. I have a small consulting company. But I'm trying to put more time in my schedule too. I've been working pretty hard at changing my life around," I said. "I'm actually writing a book about it," I told him wondering if this might be a good way to discuss the parameters of this potential friendship.

"Wow, really?" he said, stopping mid-strum. "What have you been doing to change your life?"

"Hmmmm.... Well, one major thing is that I decided not to date for a year... to um, clear my head. Yes, now I'm focusing on being friends with people."

"That makes sense," he said thoughtfully.

Talking about the book seemed like a safe way to discuss my intentions. Eventually, my fingers got too sore to play, and we packed up. "What do you have planned for the evening?" he asked.

"Nothing much," I said wondering where this was going.

"Do you want to get a bit to eat?"

"Uh, sure... How about Mexican?"

"Sure, I like any kind of food," he said.

Over Mexican food, we talked about our lives.

"What was it like working for GM? I can't picture you working on an assembly line."

"I used to bring a book with me. I would work really fast to finish my part so I had time to read."

"What were you reading about?" I asked.

"Psychology, mostly. I love psychology. I almost got a degree in it but I switched to engineering." *That's really cool*, I thought. *I love psychology too. What a gift to be able to talk about it with someone who could actually understand what I was talking about.*

"What about you?" he asked. "You said you moved around a bit. Do you consider anywhere in particular home?"

"Boston, I guess. Southwest Florida is my home now," I said confidently. "My whole family is here. We all moved down about ten years ago."

"That's cool. Why didn't you become a scientist if that's what you studied?" he asked.

"Oh, I hated labs in college," I replied. "I couldn't imagine working in a lab? After college, I didn't know what to do, so I took three months off and did a sequestered retreat in the mountains."

"Wow, that's wild! What kind of retreat? A religious retreat?"

"Kind of. It was called the Spiritual Lifestyle Program, SLP. It was based in the yogic tradition. Actually, most people went to it for the yoga. I might bet I was the only one who went for the spirituality," I said with a laugh.

"I'm a Buddhist, myself," he said.

"Wow, I never would have guessed that. Then again, you are very chilled out, so that makes sense."

I was happy to be making a new friend, and we had quite a bit in common. But, over the next few days I had to fight the old habit of becoming consumed with thinking about a man after spending time with him. *Maybe he would make a good boyfriend...*

***

Heading to my strategic planning session with the Naples Symphony Orchestra, I got off the elevator and passed two large, abstract sculptures. *It's going to be just fine*, I thought, *just fine. Take a deep breath.* I entered the classroom and greeted the participants who were already assembling at the U-shaped grouping of tables. I set up my supplies at the first table in front.

This would be the first strategic planning session since the legendary founder and president, Melanie Dobson, had retired. It was a new era. It was said that Ms. Dobson had built the Symphony brick by brick. She had solicited donations from all of Naples' elite to construct her dream. In the fundraising community, she was considered an icon. As with many icons, she was also known for her iron-fisted control of every aspect of the Symphony. She had ruled by fear and intimidation for more than three decades.

But her rule had ended, and the new director Karen Bernstein, seemed to be the polar opposite: young, flexible and open to new ideas. When I met her, Karen had struck me as extremely smart, obviously well-educated. She seemed very much at home in the polished, elite atmosphere of the Symphony. Although her hair was cut strikingly short in a very no-nonsense style, she wore cutting-edge, artsy jewelry.

When we had met the week prior, Karen had discussed her desire to create an inclusive planning process, which would set the direction for the organization for the next few years.

"I would like you to work with the management team to come up with some general areas of focus or 'buckets' to provide to the board of directors. The board will then further refine them and create the actual strategic plan in the fall," she had said.

I had put quite a bit of thought into the event. I had never worked with an arts organization, and I did a lot of thinking about the role they played in the community.

While I worked with the Symphony's IT guy, Dave got the audio visual equipment in place, I worried that hives were probably creeping up my neck. I was a little intimidated by the whole thing. I had conducted many operational planning sessions in my past position as chief program officer and had done a few visioning and planning exercises with clients, but this would be my first full strategic planning session.

After getting the audio/visual equipment situated, I opened the workshop. "Welcome, everyone. I'm really looking forward to today's workshop. I always like to start out any kind of meeting by getting to know people personally. So, let's go around and tell a little about themselves: what your position is, how long you've been with the Symphony and one thing that makes you special."

As each person shared a little about him or herself, it was obvious that there was a lot they didn't know about each other.

"Really? You restore vintage automobiles? I had no idea!" the CFO said to orchestra director.

"When it was my turn I said, "I'm Geva. I grew up in Boston and I'm happy to say I'm from southwest Florida now. And something that makes me special is that I am learning to play the guitar, and I play the drums." A few people clapped to hear that I was a fellow music lover.
"It's really important to understand what kinds of thoughts and feelings everyone is bringing into the planning process. So, tell me how you feel about strategic planning."

No one wanted to answer. "Okay," I told them, "there is no right or wrong answer."

Finally, the programs director said "Well, frustrated, I guess."

"Why is that? Frustrated because you're here on a Saturday?"

"No, I guess I'm frustrated because in the past we've made strategic plans and no one ever did anything with them."

"The director didn't even attend the meetings." someone else said.

"The plans were meaningless and it feels like a waste of time."

"I understand how you feel," I said looking at them. "It would be very frustrating to put a lot of time into something and then not have anything come of it."

"However," I went on. "There are two things I want to mention. First, part of the value of planning is what takes place in the room. It's the conversation and creativity and what you create together that counts. And a lot of the things you're going to talk about today, you're going to be able to put in place. Important things will come out of this process that won't require board approval. You'll be able to implement it yourselves. Obviously, the big ideas that come out, you'll need to get board approval on. But, a lot of day-to-day changes you'll be able to implement yourselves." The group looked visibly relieved.

"And there's one other thing. In the past, you didn't have the support of the director for the ideas you came up with. She wasn't even there. Well, take a look. Your director's sitting right over there," I said. pointing to Karen. Anything you come up with together and agree upon, I'm sure she will advocate for," Karen smiled, and there was a comfortable feeling in the room.

Over the course of the day, I used a variety of activities to spark their thinking and open their minds. I tried to use my standard model of visioning, followed by figuring out what steps are necessary to reach the vision, but it proved challenging. Standing at the white board, we fleshed out what the group felt society and the community should look like in the future. Then I asked them to describe society as it is now.

"Disconnected," one person said

"Isolated," a woman in the back said

"Busy" Karen said.

"Stressful" the conductor said.

"Okay, now let's talk about how the Symphony can help create that ideal vision," I said.

We made some headway. But, the group had a hard time figuring out how the Symphony played a part in shaping society. I had them describe the guests' experience. "First, who are your guests? Describe them."

"For the concerts our guests are mostly upper middle class... For the other events it is a mix," the program director said.

"Wealthy... most of our guests are fairly affluent," the conductor said.

"And what is the experience like? Describe how the experience feels when they visit the Symphony," I said.

As they described the experience, one word that stuck out was "transcendent." The guest experienced a transcendent experience.

"So, do you see value in this? Do you see how this kind of experience affects the community and our society?"

"Well, kind of..." one person said.

It was clear that as an arts organization, the Symphony no longer had a clear understanding of what problem they were established to solve. Or perhaps the needs of society had changed since the organization had formed.

"I don't think that arts organizations serve the same purpose as social service organizations," the development director said sternly. Her arms were crossed in front of her, and she looked as though the entire conversation felt challenging to her. "We are not providing food or shelter. What we provide is an enrichment to life."

I had put a lot of thought into the role of an arts organization. Although most of my other clients delivered direct services like working with the homeless or serving veterans, I was convinced that arts organizations served a vital, if poorly-understood role in society. Together we had to figure it out.

"I can see how you might look at it that way. However, the government doesn't give out 501c3 tax status easily. They give it out because an organization is providing a service that they cannot. In this way, you are working as a partner with the government to improve society," I said. "What role do you think you currently play in the community?" I looked around.

"Well, our role is to provide high-quality programming to the community," one person said confidently.

"Part of our role is to be leaders, to lead the community,"

"That makes sense. I can see how you believe it is your role to be kind of cultural leaders by bringing quality programming to the community. But, what I'm starting to pick up on is that the organization sees itself as somewhat separate from the community," I said. "I want to invite you to start seeing yourself as part of the community. You and everyone else make up the community. The community is not some abstract thing outside of yourself, it is something you are a part of." About half the room looked skeptical. The other half seemed intrigued by the idea.

"This is just to get you to start to think about these ideas. You don't have to accept them. I just want to stimulate your thinking. But right now, I want to show you part of a movie that has to do with the importance of music in a community."

The film "The Singing Revolution" is about how hundreds of thousands of Estonians risked their lives by gathering to sing forbidden patriotic songs, which ultimately united the country in its quest for independence. My point was that the organization could in fact play a role in bringing the community together, one of the most needed services, currently.

After breaking for lunch, several people commented on how the film had touched them. After we resumed the session, I had them pair up and discuss different segments of a report produced by the League of American Orchestras, which was a visioning document for orchestras broken into sections on internal culture, community relationships, artistic activities and financial structure.

"Okay, let's come back together, everybody," I said. "This is a visioning document I came across that a group of symphonies put together to help arts organizations all over the world.

"Carol, you and your partner discussed community relations. What did you get out of the report?"

"One part that really struck us was this one," she said, holding up the paper in front of her to read aloud "What if a community viewed its orchestra as the infrastructure of music in the community rather than exclusively as a provider of concerts?" She looked up momentarily, and then continued "...and allowed the unique capability of the individuals of the institution to be used to help the organization be more responsive to community needs?" She paused and then continued, "We thought that was interesting, especially based on our conversation before the lunch break. We could start to see ourselves as the infrastructure for music happening," she said, looking at her partner Jennifer.

"Yes, we also talked a lot about demographics and how the community is changing," Jennifer said. "There are a lot more year-round residents now. We need to be sensitive to that."

"And a lot more Hispanic residents. We need to serve their needs better as well," the education director piped in.

We went on to discuss the other areas of the report, which contained some concrete examples of how to build a world-class symphony that truly served the community. I summed up. "I'm going to take the notes from our discussion and create the framework for a plan. You can then add to it, edit it and provide it to the board of directors for their input. So, do you have any questions or thought s you'd like to share?"

"I feel really good about the discussion. I never really looked at our organization this way before. I especially liked the part about our being partners with the government to improve society. I feel... energized," the programs director said.

"Thank you all for your participation today," I said, smiling.

As I walked back toward the elevator, I felt tired but satisfied. *I could actually make a substantial impact on this organization in one day and then move on. Where will they be in a year? Will they implement any of it? Or will they stick to their past way of thinking? Will they help re-build our broken society? At least they listened to me and I got them to consider some important concepts.*

***

Jeanie and I were stretched out on yoga mats on the big lawn in front of the amphitheater. We were doing yoga before drum practice but kept stopping to talk. George and Starbo were up on the stage practicing about forty feet away.

"When did you first learn yoga?" I asked.

"Oh, I can't remember. But I did my yoga teacher training about ten years ago in the Bahamas?"

"At the ashram down there?" I asked, thinking of a center I had heard of.

"Yep. It was a month-long program. Amazing. Yoga three times a day, vegetarian food, the beach..."

"Sounds awesome. Hey, listen There's something I wanted to ask you about," I said, turning over on my stomach.

"Sure, what?"

"George and I hung out the other day... and I enjoyed it," I said.

"So?" She looked confused.

"Well, I enjoyed it."

"And, so, what happened? What are you not telling me?" She moved into table position. Even though we hadn't spent that much time together, I felt like I could tell her about my concerns.

"Nothing... nothing happened. I just enjoyed it is all," I said feeling defensive.

"And what's wrong with that?" She still looked confused.

"I guess I'd like to have more of it on a regular basis," I said, wondering if something was wrong with me. I got into table position as well.

"So? I don't see the problem." She leaned back and stretched her arms out in front of her.

"I don't want to need someone, but I really like that he's so in the moment, no agenda, nothing else on his mind." I lay down in shavasana or corpse pose to relax.

"I still don't see the problem," she said lying down next to me. I couldn't articulate why wanting or needing to be with someone bothered me so much, but it felt good to get it off my chest. Even though she was so different from me, I felt comfortable talking to her. *Maybe I like her because she is so different from me. She really doesn't seem to care what anyone thinks. Jeanie just does her own thing....*

The next morning, I was just waking up when it occurred to me that I don't want any male to be the cornerstone of my life. I don't want my ongoing happiness to be dependent on a man's presence. I feel okay with spending time with George, but not on a regular, scheduled basis. I figured if I did that, my focus would shift.

As I lay there, the concept of "center of gravity" came to mind. I first learned about it in physics class, probably in high school, but definitely in college. The center of gravity is basically the equilibrium point within an object or between two objects. When looking at a single person, the center of gravity is at a center point within that person's body.

Classical physics states that if there are two objects considered, the center of gravity is equidistant from them and if there is a difference in mass (weight) then the center shifts toward the heavier object. My theory was that regarding people, if there was no attraction between them, each individual would retain their own center of gravity within their respective bodies. If there was a difference in attraction between the two, it would affect the location of the center of gravity. The person with the stronger positive charge would pull the center of gravity away from the person with the weaker or negative charge.

I realized this was probably the case for me in relation to dating. Over the years, my center of gravity was consistently outside myself in relationships. I always felt like I had no control in romantic involvements. My charge was weak and theirs was always strong. *Why was that? Why did I always feel like I needed a man in my life?*

I was sitting in a booth at a cafe called Healthy Planet writing, as was becoming my custom on Sundays. I was describing the center of gravity and thinking about the fact that everyone has one, when I looked up and suddenly my awareness was no longer on the few people in front of me and next to me, but included the whole room. I was aware of every single person in the room at the same time. It felt like each person was a separate planet in a solar system. Each had their own center of gravity. They all seemed suspended in time and space for a just that moment.

When they started moving again, it was as if I could still see each of them in their places, but now it all made sense. They were moving in complete harmony, the way planets orbited the sun. This shift in awareness happened quickly and then it was over and gone. I wasn't sure yet what it meant. I sat back down to absorb the sensation. *That was strange,* I thought. *What did that mean? I had absolutely no idea. Oh, it's probably nothing...*

Chapter Thirty-seven
Research

August

I knew I was making progress, but I wanted to regroup and take a step back. So I decided to research some of the main premises of the experiment. All along, I had wanted to know whether dating (and pairing) was a socially imposed construct or something else, something inherently natural. I decided to start with the work of Helen Fisher, the anthropologist I had seen in the TED Talk.

Fisher contends that "being in love is universal to humanity; it is part of human nature." This statement makes it seem that being in love is some intrinsic truth or goal. However, the Oxford English Dictionary defines human nature as "the general psychological characteristics, feelings, and behavioral traits of humankind, regarded as shared by all humans." My feeling is that just because psychological characteristics are shared does not mean they are inherent.

My interest was in looking at to what extent characteristics, feelings and behavioral traits are socially determined and to what extent they are biologically determined. *And what role does awareness play in overcoming human nature?* I ordered four of Fisher's books from Amazon. In *"Why We Love,"* Fisher says that being in love is caused by the interaction of neurotransmitters in the brain, basically causing a state of addiction.

If addicts can effectively overcome addiction to things like drugs, food and sex, one should be able to use similar methods of recovery in overcoming the state of being in love or "person addiction," as I will call it. Fisher describes stories of romantic love from all over the globe and all throughout time. In order to test her theories she designed a survey, which was distributed to men and women at and around Rutgers University and the University of Tokyo, in order to learn about romantic love.

Fisher studied the chemistry and brain circuitry of romantic love by scanning the brains of people in love. She was particularly interested in the interactions of dopamine, norepinephrine and serotonin. "Elevated levels of dopamine produce extremely focused attention, unwavering motivation and goal-directed behaviors." It is also associated with learning about novel stimuli, preference, favoritism and ecstasy. Dopamine drives up levels of testosterone, which induces lust. However, as levels of dopamine rise, levels of serotonin lower. Lowered levels of serotonin are associated with obsessive compulsiveness, hence continual thoughts of the beloved.

Fisher used an MRI machine to look at each subject's blood flow while looking at a picture of their beloved. The findings indicated that the caudate nucleus becomes active when we look at our beloved. It is a part of the ancient "reptilian" brain, located right in the center. The caudate helps us detect and perceive rewards, discriminate between rewards, prefer a particular reward, anticipate rewards and expect rewards. In addition, the vental tegemental area is activated, which contains a large number of dopamine-making cells.

Being extremely focused would seem like a positive characteristic of being in love. But, in thinking about my relationship with love, I believe it led me to focus consistently on whatever man I was dating. I would only be interested in "him" (fill in the blank with the name of any current object of my obsession) to the detriment of my family. During this time, relations with my family would become loose. I would see them infrequently. They were like secondary characters in the play that was my life. Whoever I was dating had the lead role.

The addiction to dopamine led me to "concentrate relentlessly" on the positive qualities, while ignoring the negative ones. This was certainly true with Carlos. I ignored his wandering eye and ignored what my gut instincts were telling me all along. I focused on that one amazing week in Mexico and the promise of a wonderful future, while ignoring the reality of what my gut was telling me every day: that I was with someone who could not be trusted.

"Goal-directed behavior combined with the relentless concentration is what leads people to think that the object of their affection as unique," Fisher writes. I had always wondered why it was that I could date so many different kinds of men and still find them to be unique and wonderful. Now seeing that the real addiction was not to an individual, but to love itself, was a revelation. I was in love with being in love. I needed the high that comes with being in love in order to feel okay, to feel safe. This is why when one relationship ended, I was immediately searching for a replacement.

The role that serotonin played in the whole thing was certainly central. As dopamine levels rise, serotonin lowers. Serotonin is the neurotransmitter that makes us feel content and calm. According to Fisher, persistent, involuntary, or irresistible ruminations about a sweetheart are associated with low levels of serotonin. As serotonin lowers, it causes feelings of anxiety and insecurity.

I remember being supremely content with Bryan on the weekends, but anxious and depressed when we were apart during the week. It made sense that while I was with him, my dopamine levels rose due to the excitement and...the sex. But, because dopamine is antagonistic to serotonin, after leaving on Monday mornings, my serotonin levels plummeted and I missed him terribly on Tuesdays and Wednesdays. By Thursday I could start looking forward to the weekend.

It had to be more than sex, love and addiction. *What is behind the addiction? Why are women addicted to men?*

***

The next day, I sat at my desk trying to write. But I kept thinking about love and addiction. *Why do women need men in their lives? I thought. Why do we need them more than they need us?* I grabbed a piece of paper to jot down my thoughts. *Why do we have to get married?* I wrote. *What would life look like without marriage? What do they have that we need so badly that it throws off our center of gravity?*

Does it have to do with supply and demand? Maybe economics has the answer. Are there more women than men? No. Do they provide more in the relationship than we do?

I made two lists to compare what each sex provides in a relationship:

Men -

shelter
protection
income
sex
children
a fantasy

Women -

companionship
status
cooking
cleaning
sex
children

My Woman list seemed a bit outdated. *Are we still expected to cook and clean?* I wasn't sure. Sex and children were on both lists so they cancelled each other out. It looked like it came down to money, but that didn't make sense. We make our own money now.

I decided to see what Google had to say. *Okay Google,* "Why do women need men?" There were 1.2 billion responses. *Hmmmm...* "Why does a fish need a bicycle?" read one response. After about an hour of searching, I read an article that made me feel like a bomb had dropped on my mind. It was written by Joseph Pleck, PhD, a contributor to NOMAS, the National Organization of Men Against Sexism.

In the article Pleck effectively described a complete system that had existed under my very nose for my entire life and of which I had been completely unaware. Pleck described the power dynamics that operate between men under patriarchy, including the intricate hierarchies that are created. Apparently, men's power with other men is determined by an elaborate hierarchical system that all men are all aware of, but do not talk about directly.

Power within the various levels of the hierarchy is determined by criteria related to masculinity. The definitions of masculinity vary according to individual societies, but across the board they are related to age and physical strength. In the United States, the ability to earn money (and to a lesser degree) success with women are added.

According to Pleck, the division between gay and straight men is extremely important to maintaining the hierarchy. This is because it provides straight men with a stark example of a lack of masculinity. Therefore, to be gay receives negative consequences calling a man "gay" is a weapon of choice. The less gay a man is perceived and the more masculine, the more privileges he receives under this power structure.

Under patriarchy, women serve several purposes. To men, women are symbols of success in their competition with each other. *With Each Other... Ah, it is all falling into place...* Women also provide a mediating role in society. Pleck suggests that if men were left to their own devices, they would rape and murder each other. Having women around lessens their anxieties and provides "social lubrication."

Women also play another important role in patriarchal politics. They *(we?)* provide a space of refuge for men to retreat to after dealing with the stresses of the daily struggle with other men and the relentless competition with each other. We provide a soft place for them to rest and recuperate their psyches. *How come nobody tells us this?*

And finally, and most importantly, women play the role of the underclass to men. Women represent the lowest possible level in society - a level to which a man can never fall. Competition among men may be fierce, but it is somewhat ordered by the presence of women as the ultimate underclass. If women were made 100% equal, the pool of competition would double and so would their anxieties, Pleck wrote.

I sat back, stunned. The silence of the room seemed to echo around me. *How had I not known about this elaborate system? It made perfect sense!* Images kept flashing through my mind - Standing with two men as they inconspicuously sized each other up. *How many times had that happened?!* Sitting in business meetings where men seemed to be talking across each other or about slightly different subjects...

Men had always seemed like a foreign species to me. I could never understand why they did what they did, why they said what they said. But now, it all added up... They were competing against each other in a system that I was completely unaware of, every minute of the day. But, how did that relate to the original question, "Why do women need men?" Well, that seemed obvious. *If the whole power structure of society revolves around men... and women are the lowest class... and women as a class have no power... then women need men to have power in society. The power is through association with men.*

I sat back in my chair. *Everything in society reinforces this concept.* In countless ways the system was being kept in place. Entire industries were created to help women try to outshine each other in order to capture a man's heart, and thereby grab a little piece of (borrowed) power.

If a woman is not married, she does not fit into the power structure at all. No wonder I was feeling so much pressure to get married. As I got older, I must have subconsciously recognized the need to secure some power in my own life... or fit into the structure... and the only way to do that was to get married. This is why women are addicted to men and dating in society.

***

Journal Entry: 8-7-2012

My guitar playing seems to be improving, slowly but surely. Now that my schedule has changed, I have more time to practice. This morning while I was practicing, I noticed some improvement. I'm starting to see a relationship between the notes and the sounds. I've started to look at the process as not just a matter of needing more practice, but needing to build the physical synapses in the right side of my brain. It's not about ability and it's nothing personal. It's simply a matter of not having used the right side of my brain for 25 years and the necessity to build the synapses.

Chapter Thirty-eight
A Walk in the Sunshine

We had pulled four little cafe tables together to make one long one. Under the fluorescent lights of the sandwich shop, the scene felt a little surreal. Here I was, seated between my college Bio Club friend Anne on my left, and Donna on my right. George was across from us. All around us were other members of the Fort Myers Drum Circle. My mind tried to rationalize how it was possible that these two worlds could be colliding, but it was something like in those movies where the person travels back in time and meets up with their former self. Some kind of cosmic shift might occur.

Anne had friend requested me on Facebook after hearing from Samantha that I was living in Florida. It turned out that she lived one town away in Fort Myers. We had met up at the farmer's market drum circle, and then everyone decided to go out for lunch.

"So, you guys went to college together?" George said looking curious. I could tell he was trying to do the math, since Anne was about 15 years older than me.

"Yes, we were in the Bio Club together," I said, letting him wonder a while longer. "Anne is a naturalist now. She takes people on tours of the Everglades."

253

"Wow, that's really cool," he said smiling.

George and Anne were sitting next to each other and I wondered if they would hit it off, seeing that they were close in age. But neither seemed to notice the other.

"George, UMass is a commuter school. They cater to the 'non-traditional' student. That's why we were in the same class," I said.

"Oh, I see," he said, looking up from his sandwich. "How do you like being a naturalist?"

"It's great so far," she said. "I love being outdoors for a change. Sometimes, the tourists can be a bit much, but it's cool for the most part."

After lunch, our group dispersed and I turned to Anne. "Hey, it was so good to see you. I hope you'll come and drum again." I felt a little awkward because Anne and I hadn't seen each other in so long. We probably had a million things to catch up about, but George and I had made plans.

"Yes, definitely. I'll have to buy a drum sometime. Anyway, let's keep in touch," she said.

George and I went to the Calusa Nature Center. After visiting the exhibits, we watched a film in the planetarium about NASA's IBEX project. As I sat there under the big dome, I wondered *Am I on a date? Am I cheating on my own experiment?*

The film that was projected onto the inside of the dome was thrilling. I learned that our solar system is actually a bubble of charged particles, hurtling through the universe. The charged particles come from the sun, and protect us from the harmful particles in outer space. It felt good to have someone sitting next to me, who was likewise interested in such facts. Normally, I would want to snuggle up to the man I was with when in a movie theater. *We're friends. Just friends.*

"What do you want to do now?" George asked as we left the theater.

"Hmmm... there's a boardwalk out back. We could go for a walk," I suggested.

"Okay, you lead the way."

The afternoon sun lit up the greenery on either side of the meandering trail as we walked along. *Wow, this really feels like a date,* I thought. Although we had discussed keeping things on a friendly basis, I could not help but notice the charged air.

"How's the guitar coming along? Have you been practicing?" He looked over at me quizzically.

"A bit," I said sheepishly. "Look at the angle the boardwalk makes just as it turns. I'd like to draw that," I said trying to distract him.

"Wow, you draw too!" He seemed surprised.

"Yeah, not much lately..." I replied. *People usually hold hands on such a romantic stroll*, I thought. I thrust my hands into the pockets of my jeans. *No! We are just friends... just friends...*

"I wish I could draw. I can't even draw a straight line," he said.

"Oh, I believe everybody can draw. It's just a matter of seeing," I said, looking at the sky. "Drawing doesn't take place in your hands. It takes place in your eyes."

"I don't know," he said, doubtfully.

"You could learn if you wanted to. I'd be happy to teach you," I said. *What?! Now you're going to teach him how to draw! Geva, get a hold of yourself!*

"We'll see," he mumbled.

After an awkward silence, I said, "Hey George, I read this really interesting article the other day about patriarchy."

"Yeah, what did it say?" I repeated what I had read.

"Yep. That's pretty accurate. That pretty much describes what it's like to be male," he said, with a little smile.

"What?! I can't believe it! How can this entire system exist and nobody knows about it, nobody talks about it?" My outburst broke up the silent, serene atmosphere.

"Well, I don't know, but that's the way it is. Men always compare themselves to each other and they always compete. They probably do it right in front of you and you don't even realize it."

"Yeah, I think so," I said, feeling foolish. I was really glad we were just friends, so we could actually have meaningful conversations like this. If we were dating, we probably never would have talked about things like patriarchy.

The boardwalk circled around and eventually we were back at the beginning. "That was really nice. I'm glad we did that," George said smiling.

"Me too," I said feeling somewhat relieved that we had successfully completed the journey without anything romantic happening.

***

Journal Entry: 8-15-2012

I don't know what I think or feel about George. Sometimes, when he's not around, I wonder what it would be like if we were romantic. It seems natural, considering we get along pretty well and have so much in common. I'm not sure there is chemistry there though. He feels like a brother, someone trustworthy. He's so smart and interesting...Could there be more?

***

When I arrived at Riverside Park, George said, "Jeanie and Starbo are running late."

"What? How late are they going to be?" I was irritated that I had rushed to finish work and rushed to arrive on time.

"They'll be another half hour," he replied. We were leaning on his black Miata.

"Hmmm... what can we do?" I said, looking around. I didn't feel like sitting on the stage of the bandshell for a half an hour.

"Why don't we go see if the park actually connects to the other end of my street?" I said, pointing to the far side of the park.

We headed over the train tracks in the general direction of my street. The sun was shining overhead. "Isn't it a beautiful day, George?" He nodded.

"Yeah, I'm kind of glad Jeanie and Starbo are late. Nice day for a walk." We passed into an area with a canopy of huge oak trees, shading our walkway.

"Wow, It's so pretty here," I said.

Light was shining down through the trees, illuminating the place, creating a magical realm. It felt like a separate park. Suddenly we were in some lost, forgotten place, off the radar. There was no one around except for some teenagers hanging out off to our left. But, they didn't seem to notice us.

"Look there's a road over there" George said, motioning ahead. I noticed an old woman coming from that direction. George and I walked slowly, taking our time. The old woman seemed to be on a mission, heading straight for us. She was wearing an apron over a faded dress. Her grey hair was pulled back into a bun.

"You are sooooo beautiful..." the old woman said as she passed by, staring into my eyes. I smiled and said, "Thank you."

"And he's pretty nifty too," she said, indicating George. She continued on her mission, which apparently had nothing to do with us. She was making a bee-line for the opening in the trees we had walked though moments before.

Okay, that never happens to me, I thought. Something is definitely going on. I felt like I had steeped into another world and I didn't mean just the little park. Strange occurrences kept happening that I could neither explain nor dismiss.

***

Journal Entry: 8-17-2012

It occurred to me this morning that I usually wait for some specific inspiration to create art. Hence, my paintings have been few and far between. However, since I started making necklaces to sell, I am actually being creative - and it's because I have a reason, a purpose, a project.

Maybe I need to turn the model I have regarding art on its head. In the model I learned from my father, you make art as a private experience and then sell it. Maybe another way of looking at it would be that from the beginning it is regarded as for sale. Selling it is the reason for making it. Not that the quality would be compromised, it would still be based on inspiration. But, the purpose would be different. I can't wait to get started. How fun!

Chapter Thirty-nine
A Storm

"Hurricane Isaac was a slow-moving tropical cyclone that caused severe damage in the Caribbean and along the northern Gulf Coast of the United States in late-August 2012. The ninth tropical cyclone, ninth named storm, and fourth hurricane of the 2012 Atlantic hurricane season, Isaac developed from a tropical wave located east of the Lesser Antilles on August 21, strengthening into a tropical storm later that day. Isaac passed over Hispaniola and Cuba as a strong tropical storm, killing at least 29 people in Hispaniola, before it entered the Gulf of Mexico." Wikipedia

"Hey, Geva it's Joe Pescatrice with the Red Cross," a man's voice said on the other end of the line. *Uh oh, this can't be good. Joe never calls, especially at 9 p.m.*

"Hi Joe. What's going on?" Joe Pescatrice was a legend at the Red Cross. He had over 50 years of volunteer service under his belt, and his friendly face was known to everyone in Lee County government.

"Well, I don't know if you got a chance to look at the weather, but there's a storm heading our way," he said.

"Yeah, I saw that something was going on. Is it bad?"

"Well, we're not sure yet. There's going to be a meeting at the EOC tomorrow at 10 AM. They're going to do a briefing. Do you think you could make it?"

"Sure, no problem. I'll be there," I had only been to the emergency operations center once for training. Now, I would see it in full operation.

"Oh, that's great. I really appreciate it. I'll be there too. Remember to wear the Red Cross uniform."

"Okay, Joe. See you tomorrow," The full impact of the conversation started to dawn on me.

The Red Cross is the only organization that I volunteer with. As a consultant, many organizations had asked me to volunteer with them or serve on their board of directors, but I made it a policy early on to politely decline. I wanted to avoid any potential conflict of interest. But I had always made an exception for the Red Cross. I had become personally involved with them way before I even opened the consulting firm.

Four years prior, Tropical Strom Fay had flooded an entire trailer park, leaving the largely Hispanic community homeless. It was all over the news. There were pictures of the flood victims wading through waist-high water in the trailer park and footage of families at a shelter. I didn't realize where the shelter was located until I headed out to rollerblade behind my local community center. Signs in front stated that the center was the designated shelter.

The next time I went roller-blading, I was curious. I was thinking about the fact that the community center was now full of displaced Hispanic families, many of whom probably couldn't speak English. Because I felt a particular kinship with the Hispanic community, I wanted to know more. Inside, I found the Red Cross understaffed, straining to meet the needs of the shelter population.

I immediately signed up to be a "spontaneous volunteer." I performed a variety of tasks, including manning the kids' playroom, serving meals, and translating for clients. Usually a shelter is open for only a few days. The Tropical Storm Fay sheltering event turned out to be one of the longest running shelter operations in the history of the Red Cross, clocking in at 51 days. Finally, local officials agreed to re-open the trailer park and let the residents go home.

After that experience, I took virtually every course the Red Cross offered. I then analyzed the needs of the organization and my skills and requested to work in the Government Relations Department as a liaison. Government liaisons represent the Red Cross in the Emergency Operations Center during an emergency. They communicate back and forth between the Red Cross and government officials to make sure the shelter and feeding needs of affected individuals are taken care of.

My training consisted of four online courses, each about ten hours long. I then attended two full-day classes with the Red Cross and four full-day classes with FEMA at the EOC. I learned all about how responses to major disasters are coordinated and managed. But, Hurricane Isaac was to be my first real hurricane, and my first activation since training started four years prior. *Why now?* I thought. *Why in the middle of the experiment?*

When I drove up to the emergency operations center the next morning, cars were parked on either side of the long drive way. A man in a tan uniform flagged me past the metal speaker box, where we usually state our names and reasons for visiting. My hands gripped the steering wheel tighter. I steadied my breathing. I had to park at the top of the hill and around the back of the new emergency operations center, which wasn't open yet.

I walked down the hill in my over-sized, Red Cross tee shirt, acutely aware of the stylishly dressed military personnel walking briskly by. *Why didn't I buy a Red Cross polo shirt when I had a chance? This tee shirt is ridiculous!* A trickle of sweat ran down my side in the cool, morning air. *It's fine. Everything's fine. You are just as good as they are.*

Even though I was 10 minutes early, the command center was already filled to capacity. All the heads of county government were there, including the fire department, Sheriff's office, health department, transportation and utilities. There were about 60 people in various uniforms in their assigned seats, or standing against the wall. I was one of six women in the room. *Why did I choose Government Relations, again?*

I found a seat by the media near the front of the room. I could see Joe Pescatrice, already seated across the room, talking with someone in a dark blue uniform. Joe's short white hair contrasted with his mocha-colored skin that was neatly combed into place as always.

The EOC Manager, Jim stepped up to the podium. "Good morning. Is this thing on?" tapped the microphone. "Thank you all for being here. I know you thought we might dodge a hurricane this year, but it looks like we're not so lucky this time. As you can see from the slide on the screen in front of you, Tropical Storm Isaac is currently on a path to impact southwest Florida." He looked around the room before continuing. "At this point the hurricane could travel as far west as this," he said using a pointer to indicate the outer left part of the path. "But, there is a significant possibility that it will make landfall."

The plump man with the crew cut next to me had his arms crossed over his chest and leaned back in his chair. "What is the status of the EOC?" he asked.

"I'm glad you asked that Bob," the manager said. "We will be partially activated from 5pm today and will open to full activation tomorrow at 8 am." I wondered what that meant for me. I was supposed to be home working on the book.

"We're not as worried about an initial impact with this storm. We're more concerned with subsequent storm surge and flooding."

"Transportation is ready," said the man next to Joe. "Just say the word."

"Good, glad to hear it," the manager nodded. "All right, I will advise you all of any updates, but plan to have your reps here at 5 pm today."

As the meeting broke up, I noticed Joe making his way over to me, his white Red Cross polo with the emblem over the heart was tucked into his khakis. "Hey kiddo. Glad to see you here."

"Oh, happy to be here," I replied.

"Listen, I'm going to be down at the Collier County EOC tonight. Could you cover this one?"

"Uh, sure. No problem," I tried to keep my voice from cracking. *I have trained for this... I will be fine*, I thought looking around.

I got in my car, drove to the Red Cross headquarters, and immediately purchased two branded polo shirts. Next, I went and bought the supplies I might need for the next few days. I had started packing an overnight bag with clothes that morning just in case, but I still needed things like protein bars and dried vegetarian food. I made a list on an excel sheet for future use.

At the house, I readied for a potential hurricane. Pam was in Chicago, so I pulled the furniture off the lanai and put the yard chairs under the stairs. I brought my paintings in from the garage. I locked the door behind me, not knowing how long I would be gone. *I should probably check in with my family,* I thought.

"Mom, it's me," I said when she answered her phone.

"Hi honey, I was wondering about you. Are you coming over?"

"No, mom. I'm heading to the emergency operations center. Remember, I told you if there's a hurricane, that's where I'll be?"

"Oh yes, I forgot. With the Red Cross, right?"

"Yes, that's right. Is everybody coming to your house like usual?"

"Yes, honey. Your sisters will be arriving later. I'm proud of you."

"Thanks, mom. I'll check in with you again. Bye."

"Bye, honey."

When I arrived at the EOC, I was dressed in my polo and khakis. I signed in, found the Red Cross seat, and introduced myself to the government representatives around me. "Hi, I'm Geva," I said to the plump man in the light blue polo. The emblem said "Lee Tran," on it, which was short for Lee County Transit.

"I'm Will and this is Jose," he said pointing to the guy next to him.

"Hi," Jose said. "Is this your first time at the EOC? I see by your shirt that you're with the Red Cross, but I don't remember you."

"I did my training in this room a few years ago, but this is my first activation," I replied. Joe said to make sure to befriend the people at our table. We would be working closely together. Sometimes we would need favors and sometimes they would need favors.

"If there's anything the Red Cross can do, just ask." I said smiling. *Try to look friendly, Geva.*

"You got it. Likewise," Will said. I looked around. The room had no windows and ancient carpeting. The long tables created little islands of functional divisions like planning, management and logistics. We were a part of the logistics division. To my left were two guys from Public Safety. I went and introduced myself to them as well, and then settled in for a potentially boring five hours. My coworkers seemed genuinely nice. They seem to appreciate the presence of the Red Cross. *They probably realize that I am the only one in the room not getting paid to be here,* I thought.

The storm was moving slowly. We wouldn't know until early morning whether the hurricane would actually be a threat to Southwest Florida. Joe was supposed to relieve me at 10:00 p.m. and take the night shift. We were both wishing that the brand new EOC on the hill was open, because currently representatives literally slept on the floor behind their chairs. The new EOC had bunk beds and hot showers, but construction wasn't complete and we were stuck with "Camp Swampy."

After an hour of reading the novel I had brought and discussing the potential impacts of the storm with my coworkers, Joe called to check in.

"How's everything going up there?" he asked.

"Fine. Nothing exciting so far."

"Good, that's a good thing. Did you meet your teammates?"

"Yes, they all seem nice," I said, heading for the door so they wouldn't hear me.

"Okay, good. Well, if they let you go home at 10 pm, hightail it. Give me a call and let me know what's going on."

"Okay, will do."

The EOC remained on partial activation and would therefore close at 10 pm. I didn't have to be back until 8 am the next morning. Driving home, I felt slightly more confident. Everything had gone well. No major screw-ups. I decided to check in with my parents and see how they were faring.

"Mom, how is everything going down there?"

"Fine honey. Your father is out in the yard, boarding up the windows. Terry is helping him."

"Oh good. Do you have everything off the lanai?"

"Yes, we brought all the plants in an hour ago. We've got plenty of supplies, plenty of water. We're all set. What about you? Are you at the emergency center?"

"The Emergency Operations Center and no. They are only partially activated, so I'm sleeping at home. I'm on my way home now."

"Okay, well, keep in touch and let us know what's going on, okay?"

"Okay, Mom. Be careful. Don't let Dad work too hard... Bye."

At home, my bedroom felt foreign to me. It was so bright and airy... and feminine, in stark contrast to the dingy boy's club I had just left. After removing my uniform and setting the alarm, I fell into a deep sleep.

When I arrived at the EOC the next morning, it was fully activated. People were buzzing around, and there was a sense of excitement in the air. The chief did a briefing at 8:30 am.

"The track of the hurricane seems to be following the coast. In a moment The National Weather Service will give us an update," he said, collecting the papers in front of him. All eyes were on the large screen at the front of the room. A moderator came on the loud speaker and discussed the wind speed and rain. There was the distinct possibility of flooding in Fort Myers.

Over the next few hours, the County decided to open up shelters in two areas and requested that the Red Cross open up two additional shelters. I relayed the information back and forth, and the Red Cross sprang into action. Most of the shelters were located as much as an hour from the potential flood zone, which was in an impoverished area, and I was concerned that the residents would have a hard time getting to the shelters.

"Joe, what's the protocol for getting transportation to the residents? Can I ask Transportation to do something?"

"It's fine to ask Transportation for that. No problem."

I put the phone down and leaned across the table. "Guys, sorry to interrupt. Do you think it would be possible to get transportation for the people who live far from the shelters?"

"I don't see why not," Jose said, looking at Will.

"You would need to check with the Chief though," Jose said.

"Okay, let me check it out," *Really, I don't see why that's necessary,* I thought. *I don't remember having to get permission from the chief in our training.* Still, I headed up front to see the Chief.

"Excuse me sir. Hi, I'm Geva. I'm with the Red Cross..."

"Yes, I know. Joe told me all about you. Glad you're here. What can I do for you?"

"Well, it appears that there are a lot of residents who live pretty far from the shelters. We're wondering if it would be possible to get transportation for them," I said, trying to sound polite but firm at the same time.

"Absolutely. Make it so," he said and turned on his heel to deal with another matter. *Uh, okay... that was easier than I thought.*

When I told the Transportation guys about the approval, they called back to their headquarters for a special map. They then set up a special bus route, which would run along the coast, stop downtown, then head out to the shelters and loop back again.

I took my freeze-dried vegetarian meal out to the kitchen and ate with the other government representatives. I sat with two police officers who told me they appreciated my presence, especially considering that I was there as a volunteer. When Joe showed up at 3:00, he asked me to go to the EOC out in Hendry County. He had only just found out that as part of the Red Cross reorganization, we were actually responsible for that county as well.

My first thought was: *Oh, what a letdown. I was accomplishing things here.* My second thought was: *I HAVE TO DRIVE IN A HURRICANE?!*

"No problem, Joe," I said, trying to steady my nerves. I collected my gear, got the address and said my goodbyes.

My heart was racing as I drove to the Hendry County EOC. Wind gusts kept hitting the car, threatening to push me off the road. Palm fronds were spread out all over the highway, making for a maze. Luckily, the rain was not too hard. It seemed to be coming down vertically against the windshield. The Hendry County EOC was located down a long expanse of empty highway, with nothing but open fields all around. When I reached the gates, I had to say my name and organization into the squawk box, and the gates swung open. Inside, the brand new building seemed to be fairly empty.

I was introduced to the chief of the operation, a woman in her fifties. Over the next few hours, I worked to coordinate the delivery of over 200 meals to the local church. Strangely, during that same time, Hurricane Isaac decided it wasn't so interested in Florida, changed direction and headed for Louisiana. The rain abated and the winds died down.

The phone rang. "Hi, it's Joe," a voice said. "Looks like it's another close call. If they don't need you, you can go home." I looked down at my gym bag next to the chair.

"Okay, I'll just wrap things up and head out. I'm going to make sure the meals that are still on the way get distributed to local groups,"

"That sounds excellent. Thank you so much for your hard work, Geva. The Red Cross appreciates it. And... Good job."

As I drove back to Bonita Springs, I thought about the experience. It had ended so abruptly. *At least everyone is safe,* I thought. The sky was lightening up. *Everyone really seemed to appreciate my presence, and they listened to me. I did it. I helped out in a hurricane.* Fatigue was starting to set in, but also a small glow of satisfaction.

***

After the hurricane, or "near miss tropical storm," I kept thinking about patriarchy. There was something scratching at the back of my mind about the whole EOC situation. The EOC was very clearly a boys club. Almost everyone in there was male... and yet that's where I wanted to be in a hurricane. I remembered considering all my options when I chose a position at the Red Cross. I was trained for everything. I could have taken any position probably.

And yet when picturing myself in the middle of a hurricane, that's where I wanted to be, at the decision-center, the central location of all the military and government agency heads... the safest place around. Maybe it had nothing do with optimizing my talents and the Red Cross's greatest need. Maybe it was just the safest place around in a hurricane, the top of the patriarchal structure.

How many other times in my life had I played into the whole patriarchal structure, subconsciously? In mentally reviewing the timeline of my life, almost every choice I had ever made was impacted by the presence of that structure. I didn't realize it as I went along, but all the jobs I had taken were typically male jobs. When I went into real estate I wasn't content with selling residential real estate. I had to sell commercial real estate, customarily a man's field. When I went into haircutting, I didn't become a hairdresser. I became a barber, like my father and grandfather. It seemed that I was always trying to prove myself in men's fields, probably because that's where the power was.

Maybe that's why I never joined any women's groups. I didn't perceive any power there. What good would it do me to align myself with them? I barely understood what it meant to be part of that larger group of women. *Who the hell am I? Have I made any decisions that were purely my own, that are not based on trying to prove myself to that system? Am I even a woman?* What is a woman? Is it a mental construct? A group of characteristics that were decided upon by men in power and based on the sex organs we were born with?

I tried to think of a time when I felt truly like a woman. *With Bryan,* I thought. *Only with Bryan.* With him I could totally relax and be a woman. *Obviously! ...because he was completely a man.* As a cop, he fit into that patriarchal architecture perfectly. That's why it felt like going on vacation when I stayed at his house. I didn't have to be a psuedo-man anymore. I could just relax in the role of the woman. But is that what I want? To drop all of the power I have amassed for myself over this lifetime, and be a woman?

Chapter Forty
Friendships

September

Two days later, George and I were at Riverside Park practicing guitar. We were set up at a picnic table across from the bandshell. We were supposed to practice with Jeanie and Starbo, but she had called to say they couldn't make it. I had my back to the picnic table and was attempting to perfect the C chord, yet again. George was sitting on the stool he brought with him everywhere.

"I'm glad you told me about all that hurricane preparation stuff. Otherwise, I never would have done it."

"Even though the hurricane was a bust?" I asked.

"Well, yeah. I need to learn that stuff. Like I said, they don't get a lot of hurricanes up in Michigan..." he replied. "I really wasn't taking it seriously until you called. I didn't have water. I didn't have a radio. I didn't have canned food... If a hurricane had hit, I would have been screwed."

"No problem," I said, feeling fatigued. It had been two days since my "training hurricane" as I was coming to think of it, but I couldn't quite bounce back. The whole thing was so abrupt. One minute, I was in a high pressure room with a bunch of guys, following the course of a potentially deadly storm, and the next, I'm in Riverside Park, practicing guitar with the sun shining.

"Do you want to practice that song, "Don't Worry," that you like?" He pulled his guitar out of the case.

"Okay," I sighed.

"Wow. That's not very enthusiastic. Are you sure you want to practice?"

"Yes, I do... Really. I just have a lot on my mind," I said, getting the sheet music out of my guitar case.

"Like what? Work stuff?"

"Well, I'm kind of annoyed that Jeanie called at the last minute to cancel," I said. "I mean, she seems kind of unreliable." I suddenly felt guilty for bringing it up. She was becoming a friend.

Yeah, but that's just Jeanie. That's how she is."

"I don't think that's a good excuse. People can't just be unreliable and it expect it to o be okay with everyone else. I... I just don't trust people like that..."

"Hmmm.... Maybe you should talk to her about it. Tell her how you feel."

"Yeah, maybe," I said regretting the whole conversation.

***

The next few days were very difficult. My feelings of depression and sadness were probably partially hormonal, but they were definitely related to what was going on as well. I felt so lonely and out of control that I actually took a day off. There was a big meeting I could have gone to, but I just didn't want to. I had no food in the refrigerator, so I went and ate at a cafe. When I got home, I tried to work, but couldn't. I just watched a movie and ate icecream.

That night, I went out and looked for another skirt like my new favorite one, but the store was out of them. I was thinking about the conversation I had with George. *Why had I felt the need to go on and on about how I didn't trust Jeanie?* I couldn't seem to stop myself. I spent three hours going from one store to the next, looking for a brightly-colored, cotton skirt.

I think I really wanted George to refute the fact that I required someone to be reliable and dependable in order to trust them. He had just listened. Jeanie often changes her mind about things that she has said she wants to do. And she shows up late. I, clearly, do not trust people who act in inconsistent ways. I tried one last store. No luck. I just wanted a simple, cotton skirt. *Is that too much to ask?!*

Now Geroge is going to tell Jeanie what I said and then she's really going to hate me. Wait a minute! This feels just like high school. That's what this is about. I am literally reliving the same issues I had in high school. I can't believe it! When will I grow out of this stuff? I thought, getting into my car.

***

Journal Entry: 9-16-2012

I keep thinking about the end of the experiment. I feel like I need to come to some conclusions before it ends, especially about dating. Yesterday, I was thinking that I don't want to get involved with someone now, not even with an amazing man. I want to "hitch myself to my own star." I feel like if I got involved with someone, my focus would be completely on him and I would lose out on all the cool things that are happening and are coming up.

Chapter Forty-one
Revelations

The following Tuesday, when I pulled into the parking lot at Riverside Park, George was already there.

"Hey, how's it going?" he called out, as I ascended the steps to the stage.

"All right," I said. "Another busy day. Where's Jeanie and Starbo?" I set up my chair across from his and set the drum down.

"I think they're coming from Happehatchee today. So who knows..."

We waited about 20 minutes and I saw Jeanie's red car with the familiar gypsy drummer sign on it.

"I'll be back in a sec," I said to George as I headed to the parking lot.

"Hey! Sorry, we're late. We -" she said as I walked up.

"Yeah, about that... Um..." *Just say it,* I thought to myself. *It's not a big deal.* Why was my heart racing then? "Could you do me a favor?"

"Sure, what?" she said looking at me quizzically. "Starbo could you bring my chair?"

"Could you call and let us know when you're going to be late?" I asked, running my hand through my hair.

"Uh, sure. I got held up doing interviews," she said as we walked to the steps.

"I know. But, if you know you're going to be late, could you call? That way I won't rush to get here on time."

"Yeah, sure... No problem."

As we set up the drums, I felt like a great weight had lifted off of me. Although it might seem like a meaningless conversation to other people, it was monumentally important to me. *I wonder if she thinks I'm a bitch for saying that? In the past, I wouldn't have brought it up. I would have just swept it under the rug and gotten more and more irritated.*

I looked across at Jeanie. She didn't look pissed. *Maybe this is the way healthy people act. Maybe they tell each other how they feel and ask people to treat them well.*

***

The next day I was sitting at my desk, day dreaming. After getting over the shock of realizing that most of my life had been devoted to climbing my way up through the patriarchal structure, I thought about what it means to be a woman. Most of my identity was built around typically masculine characteristics. I prided myself on my ability to manifest things in the world and everything it took to make things happen, like being direct, project management and strong negotiating. But there had to be positive aspects to being a woman.

At the most basic level, women are the ones who bring life into the world and they often do so through tremendous pain and under difficult conditions. *That is miraculous in itself,* I thought. What could be more powerful than bringing life into the world? What about my decision not to have children? *I still don't want to have children. That awesome power is not one I want to use. There is a huge responsibility tied to that.*

But maybe birthing is also a metaphor. Maybe the power is not just in what happens after the birth. Maybe the power is also in the gestation. Gestation is an important part of bringing anything into the world. It was also the part of the process that I had focused on the least. I started to think about my uterus more. I had to Google the exact location, but once I did, I started to feel much more connected to it. Walking around I would think about the fact that within me I possessed one of the most powerful apparatuses in the world.

Not only does the uterus bring forth life, it also processes all the hopes, dreams, aspirations, emotions and feelings that a woman experiences every day. And monthly, it washes out what we no longer need or find useful. What a blessing it is to have an organ that cleanses us psychically on a continuous basis. Walking around I began to feel strength and pride in an organ I had taken for granted for most of my life. I no longer subconsciously felt like a man without a penis. I was a woman with a uterus.

I also reflected on a woman's place in the whole patriarchal structure. I really didn't like the idea that women are the underclass to men, the "lowest possible place in society," as Pleck suggested in his article. On the other hand, maybe in 2013 this is an enviable place to be. We are not part of the structure, and yet we are able to move around in it. Legally, we can hold the same jobs, vote, and do what needs to be done. What we aren't a part of is the constant comparison and having to prove ourselves. *Who wants to be part of that?!* I thought... True, I never had a mentor who helped me navigate the system. True, I had to fight for every opportunity I had. But, wasn't that better than being trapped in that elaborate system? I could do anything I wanted. *I'm free...*

I did like what Pleck said about women providing for mediation and lubrication in the system. *Women actually have a lot of positive qualities to bring to the table, especially in the areas of business and politics.* We are generally good at connecting. *I'm really good at connecting in business,* I thought. *Need to work on connecting in my personal life, but I'm actually really good at connecting for business.* I'm not a mega connector like some people, amassing hundreds of connections at multitudes of events, but when I meet someone I get to know them and they remember me.

***

Journal Entry: 9-20-2012

I don't think I want to work internationally. I want to the freedom to travel and see new places, but I don't want to be away that often. I want to continue to build a life here with my family and friends. I'm not focusing on the consulting work right now. I haven't done a newsletter in months. Focusing on the book and my art.

***

A few days later, I was sitting in the big, open courtyard at Florida Gulf Coast University (FGCU) in front of a modern-looking, ornamental sculpture with colored glass pieces strung along a thick, tubular, metal arch. I was trying to compose my thoughts about what had just occurred.

I had wanted to get some input on the concept of center of gravity. So I had tried to find the physics department at my local university. Apparently, FGCU doesn't have one. I did come across the resume of a physics professor, Dr. Michael Fauerbach, online. He supposedly had a Ph. D. in experimental nuclear physics, along with a long list of publications and accomplishments.

Something that caught my eye was rugby. I thougth I saw something on his resume about rugby, which was interesting considering that none of my friends in the physics club at UMass Boston would have ever have played rugby. I'm not sure the Physics Club members ever actually saw the light of day. They were far more interested in studying and in video games than playing a sport, especially something as aggressive as rugby.... *Hmmm, a rugby-playing physics professor. What is that like?*

282

I may have been an honorary member of the physics club. I was the only one who wasn't actually any good at physics, but what I did have was half decent social skills. I think they kept me around as some kind of ambassador to the outside world. And I had hoped that some of their genius would rub off. Physics was really hard. The exams were basically three questions, each with multi-part answers. If you didn't understand one question, you would probably fail the whole exam. The odds were not good, and subsequently, I had to take physics I three times and physics II twice.

Eventually I figured out a strategy that would work. I took physics in the summer so I could focus solely on that. Taking physics in the summer also allowed me to take it at the local community college and transfer the credit back to UMass. The community college structured the exams differently, with more questions. There, I actually finished Physics II with the highest grade in the class: B+. Of course, there were only four of us in the class, but who's counting?

I wonder what a physics-playing rugby professor would look like? Driving through the maze of buildings that FGCU had become, I thought back to my time teaching there almost ten years prior. The campus looked completely different now. Back then, I had just earned my graduate degree in international policy, and after inquiring, FGCU had invited me to create two new courses for them. One was to be called "Introduction to International Studies" and the other would be "Latin American Environment." *I was so nervous that first day...*

I parked in one of the new parking garages and set out to find the professor. Dr. Fauerbach's office was actually located in a building in which I had taught some of my classes. After finding my way past the laboratories and around a few corners, I found the correct office. The door was ajar. Walking in, I saw a balding head hunched over a computer screen. "Dr. Fauerbach?" I hesitated in the doorway. He swiveled around to face me.

"I'm Geva. We spoke on the phone," I said. But, as I introduced myself, I couldn't help but notice the wheel chair pushed up against the table next to him. He seemed to be around my age, with an almost completely bald head and eyes that twinkled from behind his glasses. *Rugby?*

"Ah, yes, that was today," he said looking at his desk calendar. "Come in. Take that chair," he said, pointing to a chair across the small room.

"You had a question about physics?"

"Yes, well, I'm writing a book and I have a few questions." I made my way over to the chair and we exchanged some pleasantries about our backgrounds before I got down to the reason for my visit.

"The book I'm writing is about an experiment that I'm doing." I felt a little uncomfortable telling him about the book. *He's going to think I'm a total crackpot,* I thought. *This subject is going to seem about as far from physics as we are from the moon. This is so important,* I thought. *I have to push past my discomfort.*

"For the experiment, I decided to give up dating for one year to focus on changing my life." Dr. Fauerbach's face registered no surprise. "One of the conclusions I'm drawing from the experiment is that when people are in a relationship their center of gravity shifts from themselves to another person. If there is a difference in attraction, the gravitational pull between them would change. I guess what I want to know is whether there is any scientific basis for this theory. Would it be possible to use principles of physics to describe this concept?"

Dr. Fauerbach was kind enough to hide any traces of disgust or condescension. He looked at his hands, folded in his lap, before speaking. "You can use anything you want to describe your theory. Your book is not a science book, yes?" I nodded reluctantly. "So you can describe the concept however you like. If I'm understanding you correctly, you're talking about the point of balance between two objects or the center of mass within one body, correct?"

"Yes, that's correct," I replied.

"First, in order for gravitational pull to change, mass would have to increase and the way physicists view mass increasing is by "getting fatter.""

"What about the energy increasing? Mass is a function of energy."

"Physics has no way of measuring an increase in energy."

I hadn't realized that. It sounded completely ridiculous that in 2012, scientists could not measure a change in energy. "What if they only *currently* can't measure it? What if they don't have the instruments or it's on a different scale?"

"Physicists only measure the force pushing down on an object."

"What if the force is not down, it's between?"

"There is no way to test it. You see, in physics the gravitational field is only in one direction, toward the center of the earth. What you are describing is multidirectional. Therefore, you cannot use physics to describe it."

"What you're saying is that while my theory may or may not be correct, I can't use physics to describe it because physics only takes into account gravity in one direction. Therefore, my concept is outside the scope of physics?"

"Yes, that would be correct." He adjusted his glasses. "If you want to explain it using physics, then you have to use the whole system."

"Okay. Would you be willing to say that in the book?"

"Yes, I would be willing to say that what you are proposing is outside the scope of physics." For some reason I was happy with that. As long as he doesn't say it's patently crazy and there are 15 reasons why it goes against the laws of physics, it was good enough for me. Let someone else prove it's true. At least I've proven that it's not untrue.

"Well, that would be fine. Thank you, Dr. Fauerbach. I'll come back when the book is a little further along... probably a few months from now."

"Happy to help, as long as you don't write that I endorsed your idea. I am happy to say that it is outside of current thinking in physics."

And with that I stood up and politely took my leave of the professor.

***

I had a slight setback at eleven and a half months. I was supposed to go hang out with George and play guitar in the park. I was driving to meet him when he texted to say that it was raining and he had decided to go home. I immediately called him.

"Hey, I got your text."

"It's raining pretty bad hard here."

"Well, do you want to come up here? It's fine here, or we could practice at my house."

"No, all my stuff is wet," he said. "I just want to go home."

I was pissed. It was my only night to have fun during the week, and he was cancelling. There was an awkward silence.

Then I said, "Okay, I'll catch up with you later."

I felt humiliated. I really didn't know what to make of it. I took it very personally that he would cancel at the last minute and didn't want to come up to my area. I tried not to think about it and let it go. I watched some funny television. That night I felt uncomfortable trying to get to sleep.

I thought about the fact that we were supposed to be just friends. If we had been dating, I would have a right to be pissed off. But because we were supposed to be "just friends," I had no right to complain. Do friends do that to each other? I didn't think so. I felt like he completely took our friendship for granted. I tossed and turned.

I woke up early in the morning with an icky feeling inside. I especially disliked the fact that this was my reaction to a man after nearly 12 months of the experiment. I am still rattled by a man's behavior.

The next morning I meditated and decided to just let it go, let my attachment to how he was supposed to act go, let my attachment to him go, just let it all go. And I felt better. I was at a meeting with a client, when my phone rang. It was him. I awkwardly turned the phone off. When I called back later, he acted like nothing was wrong, inquiring as to whether I wanted to do something on Friday. I told him I wasn't sure. I figured I should probably do just what he did, which is to just do whatever I feel like.

Chapter Forty-two
Falling Together

A few days later, I was in the car, headed for Naples, when the phone rang.

"Hey, what are you doing?" It was George.

"I'm headed to The Phil, or should I say Artis Naples? They changed their name you know."

"Oh, yeah? What's going on there?"

"It's free one Wednesday a month at the art museum. Why, what's up?"

"Oh, I just called to see if we're still on Friday." I didn't know if I wanted to make plans with him again after he'd cancelled at the last minute.

"Yeah, listen George. I wanted to mention that when you cancelled the other night it kind of bothered me. I mean I only have one free night to do something, and we had plans."

"Yeah, I'm sorry about that. I didn't look at it that way. I was all wet and I just wanted to get home. But, we should have rearranged it, somehow." He sounded sincere.

"I'll keep that in mind though. I didn't realize that your schedule was like that."

"Yeah, I know I have no right to act all weird. It's not like we're dating. But, still I wanted you to know how I felt."

"No, I appreciate it. I want you to tell me how you feel. Otherwise, I won't know, and you'll be pissed off."

"Thanks. I appreciate that."

***

I was walking through the nature trail at Koreshan State Park with my guitar slung over my shoulder. Above me the sky was blue, and around me the lush jungle forest hugged the trail. I had my shoes off so I could feel the warm sand on my feet, and a peppery fragrance rose up around me. I came to an opening in the palms on the banks of the river and sat down. I set up my bags around me.

I took out my guitar and started playing "Amazing Grace," a tune George and I had been working on. We chose it because it only had three chords: D, A and G. I couldn't quite remember the timing, and he wasn't there to correct me. As I played, I slowed down and lengthened some of the words. I started to feel the music, and the words came alive. Although, it wasn't my religion, I could feel the author's sentiments.

At one point, it felt like the vibration of the guitar was in tune with my heart. It actually felt good to play. After hating practice for so long, I was surprised to find myself enjoying playing the guitar. The words flowed out of me in time with the music, and my spirit was at peace.

After "Amazing Grace", I moved on to a reggae tune that also used D, A and G, "Three Little Birds" by Bob Marley. I added extra emphasis to a couple of words to make it my own. The way I was singing it, it sounded more like a folk song. As I sang "Don't worry about a thing," I pictured myself singing it to an audience and reassuring them that "Every little thing's gonna be alright." After several rounds of that, I started working on a tune that I was composing myself. It was a rhythm from drumming that I had turned into a strum pattern.

My fingers were getting sore, but I felt a deep sense of satisfaction. I had been there less than an hour, so I decided to continue my walk. I rounded a corner and passed a picnic area. Two women were at a table, and one of them looked up and said "I was enjoying your music." The thought that someone could actually enjoy my music surprised me.

"Thank you... You're very kind... I appreciate it." I felt myself tearing up as I continued along.

***

Journal Entry: 9-22-2012

My painting is coming along. I've started to collect inspiration as it comes along. I have a folder where I keep images that speak to me. When I want to start a painting, I go into the folder and start working with the images to find what I want to "say." Sometimes I take quite a while preparing and researching before I start painting. I'm focusing on the "gestation" part of the process.

291

***

I was leaning up against the little wall of the rooftop bar. The Fort Myers skyline stretched out all around me.

"Great party," a voice said. I adjusted my tiara and looked up to see Meredith, my sister's best friend. Meredith was our "unofficial fifth sister."

"Yeah, thanks for coming," I said. "Let me take your picture." Meredith was almost ten years younger and single. She posed for a few shots, and I couldn't help wondering if she would find as much happiness in her life as I had in mine over the last year.

Behind me on the little stage was Kirk, my guitar instructor. He was playing some soft rock and roll tunes as background music. His white cotton shirt and tan drawstring pants fluttered in the breeze. He looked up and smiled. The air was alive with mirthful conversations.

Walking back through the crowd, I greeted new arrivals. "Stuart!" I exclaimed. "Come on in!"

"Hey, Happy Birthday!" Stuart said situating himself at a bar table that George, my sister and Starbo were sitting at.

"Ann! I'm so glad you came," I hugged her.

"I wouldn't miss it," she said with a smile. "Thanks for inviting me."

"Come join the fun. They're bringing out some appetizers any minute."

"Ann, you know Jeanie and George, right?"

"Hi. Yes I remember."

"Happy Birthday, Geva," George said, getting up to hug me.

"Thanks, George. I'm glad you're here."

Just then my Mother came up with a mischievous look on her face. "Do you want to open some presents?"

"But, I told everybody presents weren't necessary..."

"Well, we got you some anyway!" I pulled a calendar out of a pink bag. "Thanks Mom." Next there was a candle set from Garan and finally a journal from Grae.

As I opened the presents, I heard a familiar song begin to fill the air. "Happy-Birthday-to-you..." My sister Garan was walking in with a cheesecake decorated with fresh tropical flowers and topped with sparklers that crackled and lit up the night. "Happy-Birthday-to-you..."

After blowing out the sparklers to cheers and applause, I said, "I just want to thank you all for being a part of this wonderful evening. I couldn't imagine celebrating my birthday with a better bunch of people."

As I cut into the cake, my Mother said "Hey, everybody! I want to make a toast." She clinked her water glass, ding, ding, ding. "Toast!" There was a hush on the rooftop.

"I just want to recognize my amazing daughter for making such a monumental change in her life over the past year. She is an inspiration to me, and I want to honor her for her efforts. To Geva."

"To Geva," someone said. I felt my cheeks flush and I tried to let the kind words and attention sink in.

"To Geva."

After cutting the gluten-free cheesecake, Jeanie tugged on my arm and said "Come on, open my present now."

"But, I told everybody..." She dragged me over to table by the bar.

"I know," she said, placing a bag with a curly bow in my hands. "I got you something anyway. It's just little stuff. Go on."

Reaching inside I could see that the bag held several items. The first was a white, cotton scarf, with Sanscrit writing all over it. "You remembered!" Jeanie had an identical pink, cotton scarf with a Sancrit design, which I had admired. Jeanie smiled.

"Go on," she said.

Next, there was a glow-in-the-dark necklace. "For the drum circle?" I asked.

"Yep. And so is that," she replied, pointing to the squishy plastic toy that glowed pink, purple and yellow when I squeezed it. The last thing I pulled out was a rectangular pad of paper.

"Thanks, Jeanie," I said admiring the assortment of fun items.

"You're welcome. I know how organized you are. So, I made a list for you on that pad," she said turning it over.

On the first page of the pad was written:

1. Meet Jeanie, Starbo and George on Tuesdays
2. Paint pictures - the earth, the air, the fire, the water, return, return, return
3. Make really groovie necklaces
4. Breathe
5. Have a great year
6. Here she drew five hearts.

"Awwwww.... You're the best, Jeanie Williamson! And that is the best birthday present ever!" I said. "Thank you so much," I tried not to show the tears.

Chapter Forty-three
The Journey Continues

October

The experiment is over... and yet it continues. I've decided to learn how to be friends with men over the next year. I am very aware of the fact that in the past I have jumped into relationships with men so quickly, that I've been unable to get to know them and to see them for who they really are. Maybe if I focus on being friends, as with George, I will be able to learn how to be friends with them. In this way, I will be able to continue my focus on my own life and work. The foundation has been created for a fabulous new year and a fabulous new life.

Chapter Forty-four
Epilogue

When we all met up at Taco Bell, Jeanie looked at the provisions in the back of my van and said, "Where's your drum?"

"Oh my God! I forgot the drum!" I said, pulling and pushing at stuff in the van. Sweat broke out on the back of my neck in the cool autumn air. *How could I forget the drum?*

"Don't worry," she said calmly. "There are loaner drums at the festival." We didn't have time to go back for it if we wanted to arrive before sundown.

How could I forget the drum?

Driving my dad's van felt like steering a boat up the highway. George was a few car lengths behind me. When I had asked him if we should ride together, he'd given me a funny look. Clearly, he was thinking of our discussion about being "just friends."

"I don't think that's such a good idea," he'd said. I was impressed that he seemed to be taking our discussion to heart. Some guys would have kept pushing.

And now, driving up the highway, Jeanie and Starbo were, *who knows where they are*? After leaving Taco Bell, we had quickly lost track of each other. *How could I forget the drum?* We were headed to a drumming festival and I had forgotten my drum. I had spent so much time planning every aspect of the trip, but had somehow forgotten the most important thing. *I must seem like a complete buffoon.*

I had borrowed my father's van because I didn't want to sleep in a tent. I put a mattress in the back and packed every supply I could think of. I had even baked special gluten-free muffins in case there was no food I could eat.

The 21st "Paralounge" Drumming Festival was held at the Camp Kiwanis in Ocala, FL about five hours Northeast of my house. The grounds consisted of a main community center, where most of the classes were held and 12 acres for camping. Vendors set up in and around the community center and the dorms were in low, separate, buildings. Camping was around the perimeter of the area under immense pine trees, draped with Spanish moss. The far side of the community center bordered a serene lake.

Feeling fatigued from the five-hour trip, I set up the van in a semi-private spot and went to meet up with Jeanie, Starbo, and George down by the lake. They were all camping in actual tents. I had decided on sleeping in the van because on my last camping experience I had ended up flat on the hard ground at 2 a.m. when my mattress had spontaneously deflated. Sleeping in the van seemed safer anyway. I didn't know any of the 300 or so people who would be at the festival and this way I could lock the doors and sleep securely.

The sound of drumming was already in the air as I made my way down to the lake. There were no events scheduled until the following morning, the official beginning of the festival. Jeanie was unpacking supplies in front of one of the two tents they had set up in front of the lake. Buoys bobbed up and down in the safe swimming area, and a tall, white lifeguard's chair looked out over the beach keeping guard over imaginary swimmers.

"Hey Jeanie, where are George and Starbo?"

"They're looking at drums in the main building. But they said they wanted to go to Conga Corner," she said, looking over her shoulder.

"What's that?" I sat down on the long cement bench next to their tents.

"Just one of the dorms where people drum when there's no "official" drum circle going on. We can head over there in a sec, if you want. I just need to set up a few more things here."
"Okay. Did you do this all yourself?"

"Starbo helped. George put his tent up in about two seconds," she said.

"What's this now?" George said, walking up. "I heard my name."

"Oh, I was just saying what a pro you are at putting up a tent," Jeanie said, smiling.

"Thanks. Hey, are we still going to Conga Corner?" he asked.

"Yeah, but Geva still needs to get a drum and Jana isn't here until tomorrow," Jeanie replied.

How could I forget my drum?! I felt like such a loser.

"No problem." George disappeared into his tent. "You can use my second drum," he came back out and handed me a smaller version of his Djembe.

"Thanks, George. I appreciate it." *He is so nice. He really would make a good boyfriend... No, wait. I need to get to know him like a person, not a boyfriend. Don't go there, brain.*

"No problem. I brought it in case someone needed one," he said handing me the drum. "I'll meet you guys over there, okay?" George said heading off with his drum slung over his shoulder.

"You know, camping like this really reminds me of living in the islands," Jeanie said.

"Really? Which islands? I didn't know you lived in the islands."

"St. John. I moved there when I was twenty three. I thought I told you that. I moved there all by myself..." She looked off into the distance. "I didn't know anyone, but somehow it worked out. That's where I met Starbo. We lived off the land for over 15 years. No electricity, no TV, no running water... in perfect harmony with nature."

"Wow! That's so cool," I said, picking up George's drum.

"Yeah, I had two small children, and we lived completely sustainably. Let's go." *Jeanie is definitely more complex than I thought. And brave.* I couldn't imagine moving to another country, not knowing anyone, with a baby on my hip.

"Listen, Jeanie, thanks so much for arranging all of this. I really appreciate it."

"Hey, no problem. I'm glad you came along," she said with a smile.

When we got to the Conga Corner there were three sets of narrow, barrel-shaped congas set up against the front of the dorm, a picnic table and chairs making a semi-circle in front of them. I sat down with my back against the picnic table and the djembe in front of me. The rhythm was good and I blended in easily. Gradually, I was able to find my own rhythm to layer on top. I was a little surprised to hear my "voice" come out in a drum circle. *Maybe it's due to the small, intimate size.* Starbo and George were sitting behind me, and seemed to be enjoying themselves as well. When I looked back, George had a satisfied smile on his face.

Gradually, people found other things to do and the circle dwindled. I set off in search of food, heading back over the expanse of lawn toward the main building.

As I entered the main hall, the fragrance of incense and leather intermingled. I passed hundreds of drums and racks of colorful clothing for sale. Just beyond, large, round tables were set up with chairs around them. People were scattered about, talking and eating. Against the wall, two doors opened into a kitchen with a long, stainless steel counter. A cardboard sign was tacked to the wall with a hand written menu. *Thank God they have rice, beans and grilled veggies.*

"This is so awesome," I said, sitting down next to George and Starbo at one of the round tables. Steam was rising off my veggies.

"Yeah, I never want to leave," George said.

"What's the first workshop tomorrow?" I asked, stabbing a grilled piece of yellow squash.

"Grey Wolf, I think," Gorge said.

"Him be good, man. Real good," Starbo said with his island accent, leaning back in his chair.

"Yeah, I'm definitely taking his workshop," George added.

"He's famous," Jeanie said joining us at the table. "You should take Jana Broder's workshop too. It's really fun, upbeat and family-oriented."

"Sounds good," I said trying to imagine the different workshops. *I can't wait for tomorrow,* I thought.

We hung out and chatted for a while longer, and then went to bed early. I set up my bed in the back of the van, just as I had planned, but somehow cold air crept in, during the night, making sleep difficult. I tossed and turned and shivered under the blankets.

I slept in late the next morning. When I finally emerged from my big, metal bedroom, I had to hunt around to find my toiletry bag. Without water, I had no way of putting my contacts in, and I had forgotten to bring my glasses. The women's showers seemed a million miles away. I stumbled across the expanse of lawn in semi-sight, feeling vulnerable without the aid of vision. After standing in line with other equally sleepy women and girls, I washed quickly, and then headed over to the lake.

On the way, people greeted me with smiles and waves. I waved back. All kinds of people were walking around. Half were fairly mainstream looking, but there were also many interesting-looking people, with colorful clothing, tattoos and dreadlocks. They seemed to be able to express themselves freely without worrying what anyone would think.

I noticed that more tents had cropped up over night, creating a little tent village along the shore of the lake. It was nice to simply relax and unwind with nowhere to go and no obligations. A gentle breeze blew through the oak trees towering above us, and Spanish moss swayed gently.

After breakfast, we picked out our spots for the first workshop. Four rows of chairs were set up in a U shape. Gradually the seats filled, until there were close to 100 people assembled. A guy dressed only in jeans and a black leather vest came out and introduced himself as Grey Wolf. He was bald and wore a goatee. He started by explaining that his workshop was on the African rhythm called Kuku, which has more than eight separate parts.

Jeanie was sitting next to me and George was a few rows back. Grey Wolf separated the room into two sides. He taught our side one of the parts and then the other side another part. I was having trouble keeping up. I looked over. Jeanie didn't seem to be having any problem. Grey Wolf had the two sides go back and forth several times.

Next, he layered other parts on top. I kept getting confused with all of the different beats, but the result was thrilling. The room was thundering with rhythms and people all around were sweating, straining and smiling. There was a final ba da da ba, ba da da ba... bah! and the workshop was over.

Jeanie and I looked at each other. "Wow," I said. "That was intense." She nodded in shock. We headed out into the sunshine. Different smells wafted through the air: sweat, smoke, incense... On our way back to the tent village, we passed a girl with a giant hoop gyrating about her hips who smiled and waved.

Back at the campsite, the sun was sparkling on the water. People were hanging out in front of their tents, relaxing and having fun.

I was looking for somewhere to put my bag and drum.

"You can put your stuff in here if you want," George said, holding the flap of his tent open.

"Thanks," I said feeling a little confused. I was tired from not sleeping well and then taking the workshop. I just wanted to crawl into his tent and take a nap. *That would be completely inappropriate,* I thought. *I can just see where that would end up...* I put my stuff in his tent and found a beach chair to sit in.

"Do you think we're going to be able to do that?" I asked George.

"What do you mean? Do what?"

"Play Kuku back home. That was amazing. Do you think we could get the drum circle to do something like that?"

"Oh, I don't know. People like to do their own thing," he said wryly.

"We could try," Jeanie said.

We debated the possibilities for a while and then I headed back to the van for a nap.

When I woke up I pulled out my journal and wrote:

October 20, 2012

I can't believe I'm here. This is so amazing! And relaxing. I haven't felt this good in a long time. I love my new life. It feels like one big adventure. I'm happy that Jeanie, George and Starbo are a part of it.

There are so many cool people here, too. A year ago, I never would have hung out with these people. I would have judged them as too "out there," too "hippyish." Not only are they genuinely nice people, but I think I may actually prefer their company. They don't ask anything of me, just that I be myself. They are open-minded ...and relaxed ...and creative ...and they don't worry about what anyone thinks of them. I hope I get to that point someday.

Even though it's challenging, I'm glad George and I are friends, instead of dating. It is helping me understand what it's like to get to know someone one step at a time, as a person. It seems like good training. I am so lucky he is interested in being friends and not just dating.

That evening, we all went back to the main hall to watch the bands. The lights were low and all the members of the first band were wearing scary, demonic-looking masks. The music was dark and earthy. A dancer came out front with glowing wings that she moved to the music. I was mesmerized as she used various glowing props to interpret the sounds.

The next morning, we got ready for Jana Broder's class in the main building. Jana's unique style and charm were evident as she walked around, engaging the audience. In her 50's, Jana wore thick, black-rimmed glasses, and kept her white hair cropped short. Her enthusiasm was contagious as she led the circle through a routine, interjecting humor as she went along. This seemed to be a different version of a drum circle, very light and fun, as opposed to the adult, intense type I was used to.

"Go-do-pah!" she said naming the sounds she was making. The audience responded with "Go-do pah!" on the drums. Everyone was having a good time, smiling and drumming, including the children. *I bet facilitating a drum circle would be a lot of fun.*

The next workshop was by a presenter named Buddy Helm, who wore an African tunic and matching pants, contrasting his pale skin and blue eyes. His short, silver hair was covered by a brimless African cap and he looked to be about 50 or so. He was seated on stage, with a Djembe in front of him. He adjusted his microphone and glasses.

"Welcome, everybody. This workshop is on the spirituality of drumming."

"Drumming allows people to connect to themselves and others," He began a soothing, rhythmic beat that we all began to follow.

"What I'm going to focus on mostly is the "down beat," and how drummers can use it to create a safe space."

His rhythmic playing was hypnotic. Buddy's background was that of a professional drummer. He played with bands all over the world. "The best drummers understand that if the down beat is strong and consistent, the dancers will come. When I was playing out in clubs, other musicians would get jealous because all the women would flock to me when I played," he said with a wry smile. "Dancers just want a good consistent down beat to dance to and after all that's why we're playing, right?"

Hmmm.... that's why we're drumming? For the dancers? How interesting. I never thought about it that way before.

Buddy described how drumming had saved him from severe depression and how he helped other people find healing through drumming. As he spoke, his gentle humor came through and he led us in several more rhythms.

Later that evening, I saw Buddy across the room. I wanted to learn more about him. I thought about what The 28 Laws of Attraction said about asking for what you want. I walked over and said, "Hello, I enjoyed your workshop this afternoon." We chatted for quite a while in the noisy walkway, and then he asked if I would like to go outside to talk. We headed down to the lake, and sat on the sand next to the lifeguard chair. The full moon shone overhead and reflected off the water.

Okay, I'm sitting on the beach with an intriguing man. Buddy stretched out on the sand and leaned back on his elbows. He proceeded to tell me all about his life and upbringing. I noticed that my brain was not spinning stories in the background. I was actually listening to what he was saying. He had an interesting life story, but I didn't feel pulled into it at all.

What could have been a romantic interlude under the moon on the beach, ended up just a normal conversation. I no longer had the desire to automatically connect with someone, regardless of the fact that Buddy was an interesting musician. He seemed more interested in talking about himself, anyway. *Is he going to ask me anything about me?* In the past, I would have been more focused on the moonlight and chemistry than the fact that we hardly knew each other and didn't really have anything in common.

After a while there was a lull, and we stood up. "Well, it was nice talking to you Geva," he said brushing the sand off his pants. "Maybe we could do it again sometime."

"Um, sure." I dug around in my purse and handed him my card. "If you feel like talking again sometime, give me a call." *You never know. Maybe we would actually get to know each other. Doubt it, but maybe...* Walking away, I felt a quiet sense of satisfaction. It was nice to have a pleasant conversation with a man on the beach without getting caught up in a bunch of mental gymnastics. I really didn't care whether we ever spoke again.

That night at the drum circle, I couldn't get the rhythm. The drummers were set up three and four deep around a bonfire. I was sitting behind Dan, who was camping next to me. He didn't seem to be having any problem. George and Starbo were drumming next to the really good drummers across the way. The beat was strong, hard, and fast, but it seemed to have some breaks in it that I just couldn't place. I tried for a while longer as various people drifted into and out of the circle, dancing around the bonfire as it crackled and illuminated the darkness. I looked down at the drum and thought *"Well, if I can't drum, I sure can dance!"*

I got up and made my way through the circle to the center. My feet sunk in and out of the sand as I reached my arms up and moved my shoulders and hips to the beat. Most of the people trance dancing, swaying back and forth, moving around slowly. But, after being so tuned to the rhythm of the drums, I couldn't help but use my whole body as an instrument, shaking it to the beat. My arms beat against the air and my knees bounced in time with the rhythm.

A drummer behind me started a delicious solo beat and I started dancing to that. Then a rival drummer across the way started another beat, and I leaned that way dancing to his beat. Because I was one of a half dozen dancers, I didn't feel like all eyes were on me. I could do whatever I wanted. For a brief moment, I wondered if George was watching. For some reason I didn't want him to see this wild side of me. *I truly want to be friends with him. Better, not to think about that,* I thought and kept on dancing.

The fire crackled and I looked deep into the flames. I felt like the fire was burning away my inhibitions. I danced until I had no more energy then made my way back through the rows of drummers. Panting, I picked up my drum and headed out.

The next morning was Sunday morning and we all gathered in the main hall for "Rhythm Church." I didn't know what to expect. Gazing around, everyone looked sleepy, but contented. Apparently, the drumming had gone on until 4 am.

The service was facilitated by Clint, the organizer of Paralounge, who came in wearing a baseball cap, with a long braid that went down his back. His deep-blue, soulful eyes looked cautious. As people gathered, there was an air of excitement and satisfaction. Pretty soon the room was full. Clint had a microphone clipped to the front of his grey polo shirt, and his arms were completely covered with tattoos.

"Welcome everyone," he said. "Welcome to Rhythm Church."

"This is a non-denominational event," He walked around the center of the circle. "It is not about religion. It's about community. It's about coming together as a community and healing each other. Something powerful happens when people come together as a group to support each other. Our lives outside of Paralounge can sometimes be very disconnected and overwhelming. This is an opportunity for us to come together as a community and connect with each other.

"Everyone comes to Parlounge from a different place and circumstances. Some are stronger than others. Some have more challenges than others. I want to invite anyone who feels that they need for some healing to come into the center of the circle. It could be for physical healing or emotional. Whatever you are carrying, just come on up here and have a seat."

Seven people got up and sat back to back in the center of the circle. I felt pretty strong, so I stayed where I was.

"Okay drummers, I want a very soft rhythm here," He turned back to the group. We tapped on our drums in a low hum.

"Didges, come on up," Clint said, as he walked around the center group. Five people carrying Australian didgeridoos stood up and began slowly circling the group in the middle. The long, cylindrical instruments made a low, growling hum.

"Didgeridoos were created many eons ago and oral history tells us that they were created to call in the dream state. Remember when you were a child, and you flew through the air in your dreams? Remember when you swam through the deepest oceans as a child? This is the dream state, and we are calling it in." As the didges passed each person in the middle, the long instruments made vibrating sounds, pulsing at their backs. "We're calling in the dream state." The drums beat in time.

"Remember the first time your parents let you drive a car... remember your first kiss? Bring all that to the surface..." The didges hummed and buzzed and spoke the mysterious messages of Aborigines walking the plains. Wooden hand instruments clacked in time with the drums, and we rode the rhythm of the group. "Okay, didges make your way back to your seats."

"We've taken the first step. We've become like children again. Life gives us everything we need," he said.

311

We continued drumming. "Next we're going to ask the shakers to come up." He went around, handing out shakers.

"Shamen used shakers to scare evil spirits away. These instruments have been used since primitive times." Different people got up and began circling the group, shaking the little instruments back and forth over each person's head. One girl, facing me with her back to the center of the group, had tears streaming down her cheeks. A man in a tank top sitting next to her swayed back and forth.

"We have dispersed negativity. Now, we need to express some beautiful energy. You know what that means," he said, looking around. "Come on dancers. Come on out here." Both female and male dancers stood up and one by one and began to circle the group.

"Drummers, bring the tempo up." The drumming became faster. Circling the group, dancers' hips moved to the beat. Arms undulated like snakes, and the beat of the drums escalated. Eventually, after a crescendo of drumming, Clint brought the intensity back down and asked the dancers to return to their seats.

"Okay, we've had the didges out here. We've brought the child to the surface. We had the shakers out. We've danced... Let's bring the energy back down. Now, we're going to circulate some good energy," he said, handing out small, metal chimes from a big box. When he came by, I took one and stood up. I joined the chimers making their way in single file around the group in the center. As I thrust the instrument forward, a little mallet made an ethereal ding! as it connected to metal.

Ding!... Ding!... went all the chimes. Out of sync and in different pitches, the chimes had a magical quality. Circling the group, I saw that many of them now had tears streaming down their cheeks. *What a privilege it is to be part of their healing,* I thought, *and how amazing that my life has changed to the point that I have something to give them. Ding! Ding! Ding!* The chimes began to overlap and interweave.

"Okay, let's bring the volume down... Chimes, let's rotate back to your seats."

As we made our way back to our chairs, the chiming diminished slowly. "This is a lot like the drum circle. The people in the middle are like the fire. People in the middle stand up... Stand up fire... Reach up to the air and stretch it out. Okay, everyone else place your hands in front of you. Send your love into the far. That's right. Breathe in deep. Think the most beautiful thought you can think of. Breathe it out. That's right. Fire take it in... Okay, let's have a moment of silence." We stood in silence and I could feel the positive energy vibrating in the room. I wished good healing for the people in the center.

"Now, I want everybody to take in the good energy that we've created here. Take it in. Take all of the good energy in and now send it back out into the world. What we've created here is available to you every day. What we've created is community. You are a part of this community and you are part of the greater community of the world. Thank you for being part of this experience, and I'll look forward to seeing you all in the spring."

***

Journal Entry: October 13, 2013

Today is Wednesday, which means it's a writing day. I thought that since this is the last journal entry in the book, I would try to describe how my life has changed since the experiment. I'm sitting at my desk, looking out at live oak trees, covered in moss that sways in the breeze. About 5 months ago, I moved into this beautiful, sunny apartment that takes up the top floor of a two-story building. I have windows on all sides, with trees all around and a deck off the back. I call it "my little tree house." The apartment is decorated in cream, yellow, pink, and light blue, and there is art hanging in every room. One of the two bedrooms is a large, office/studio in which all kinds of creativity happens.

As far as dating goes, the year after the experiment was about learning to be friends with men. George was very helpful in that regard, although we don't spend much time together these days. He has become something of a local rock star, and doesn't have much time. As October of 2012 approached, I became more and more apprehensive about "officially" returning to dating. But I realized that I no longer possess a strong desire to date. Several men have approached me, and so far only one has been of interest. We'll see what happens. In any case, I have become so completely enamored with my own projects, friends, activities, and life, that I could really care less about pairing off. The juiciness of my life calls me on a daily basis, and it has truly become a rich experience.

My consulting work is no longer the focus of my life. I still do consulting, but I no longer seek the work. Somehow it just comes. I haven't done any marketing in over a year, and yet I now have more work than ever before. Because I have some steady contracts, I am in the lucky position of being able to choose which projects I want to work on. I no longer stress out over whether clients follow my advice or not, because consulting is not the main focus of my life. Their actions do not determine my happiness. I now enjoy the consulting that I do and the clients seem to enjoy it as well.

Two days a week are devoted to art. I have been working on a series of paintings related to women's empowerment. Some of them are in done in acrylic, a medium that I am comfortable with. Lately, I have been learning about graffiti and street art painting styles, and I have been lucky enough to find a mentor. We met on Facebook and this complete stranger has gone out of his way to teach me the finer points of graffiti. Not only is my mentor a true master, having created many beautiful works of art both on buildings and on canvas, he is an excellent teacher. His patience and persistence with me as I have made fundamental mistakes is most humbling. The fact that he is a happily married man who takes a half hour here and there out of his bus life to assist someone he has never met, restores my faith in humanity.

Yesterday, I started my second graffiti piece and as I stared at the canvas with trembling hands, thinking that it would never work, I was calmed by the thought that I had a mentor out in cyberspace who had taken the time to write out each step of the process and who would be there if I screwed up. Something else that I have come to realize is that almost anything can be fixed in painting, and in most things in life. Recently, I actually painted over a mistake I'd made with black paint - and it worked!

I spend a lot of time thinking about marketing this book. I've chosen to publish it myself, which means creating a platform for distributing my message. I have played with many different ideas and am leaning toward discussing the book with small groups and at speaking engagements. This seems like the most effective route, but has led me to focus a lot on opening up in preparation for such experiences. For me, writing the book and conducting the experiment kept overlapping. In many ways, the experiment was about learning to express myself. And as I wrote the book, I had to continually open myself further to talk about what had actually occurred. And now, marketing the book is giving me the opportunity to open up even more.

About six months ago, I took over a poetry club. With club members' consent, I expanded the group to include other artistic genres. We have our own small events and also attend large music, art or poetry events. I have enjoyed cultivating this community of creative people. We renamed the group the "The Creative Life." Some of the members have even stepped up and started organizing events. Last night I attended a music jam where I got to play guitar with several talented musicians.

One constant source of inspiration and support has been Jeanie. She has turned out to be a great friend, always up for an adventure and always there with a word of advice or inspiration. Another source of support has been my writing coach, Dawn. We've met on the phone weekly and she has managed to pull my real voice right up and out of me. Without her advice and patience, this book would not be a reality.

Probably the biggest difference since the experiment ended has been in the way that I think. I no longer spend the majority of my time thinking about men, marriage and the future. I now think about interesting things like art, music, poetry, how the world works, psychology... You name it. All sorts of interesting ideas fill my head. New understandings come to me on a regular basis. I'm able to see connections between seemingly disparate subjects and ideas. I am finally inhabiting my own brain.

Understanding that I had been trapped in addictive thinking led me to many conclusions that I am looking forward to studying further, such as the fact that addiction is not what we think it is. An addict is not some filthy guy lying in the gutter, desperately looking for his next fix. Addiction is common to all human beings. Addiction comes from an attachment to dopamine that is produced in the motivation center of the brain. It's what motivates every single action and every single thought. We are all addicts.

We are addicted to so many things it's mind-boggling. And it's not just the big things like: money, love, security, power and sex. It's also things like coffee, sugar, TV, Facebook, being right, being broke, being in control. Every single thought we have is because of an addiction rooted in our subconscious.

The good news is that when we become aware that this is how the brain works, we are no longer controlled by it. When I first realized that the reward center of my brain was controlling my thinking, it was as if, suddenly, there was total quiet. I hadn't been able to achieve that level of quietness in decades of meditation. My consciousness was finally able to step back and shut off that loud machine.

Just knowing how it worked allowed me to finally have control of my brain. Okay, my brain is not quiet like that all of the time. I have to make an effort to be aware of what is motivating my thinking. And sometimes, I just let my brain do its thing. Other times, I take the time to slow down and shut it off. I'm then able to see what ideas and beliefs are causing all the thoughts. Then it gets quiet and that's when the connections come. That's when the deep realizations happen.

One of my greatest realizations is that this experiment is not just about me. Any woman (and every woman) could benefit from taking time out of the relentless pursuit of society's perfect life to find her center of gravity. If you are reading this right now and you would like to change your life, know that you too can take the following steps:

- *You can take a break from dating for as long or as short as you like*
- *You can explore what makes you happy by trying new activities*
- *You can make new friends by reaching out and opening up*
- *You can invest in your growth by scheduling time for your own interests*

However, as important as the changes are above, they are mostly external. The most profound changes that happened for me during the experiment were internal. I worked through issues from my childhood that were holding me back. I faced problems I had with my family, and improved my relationships with them. I built better boundaries. But, most importantly, I took a look at who I had become as a person: a tired, basically miserable person, and I determined to become happy.

I hope the experiment inspires you to improve your life. But it is not a recipe for success. What makes you happy is going to be different from what makes me happy. Your current life and background are different from mine. You will have to look at yourself and your own life to determine what needs to be done. You might want to start out small and take baby steps. You might want to start out big to jump start things. It's up to you. It's your experiment now.

Once you have done all of the above, and your reserves are full, you may find your cup spilling over. You may start to hear that siren call to service. Know that your unique gifts as a woman are definitely in demand. Our world is in complete disarray. The patriarchal system has left us with an environment in peril, greater economic inequality than ever before and our food supply threatened.

But, we women excel at the soft skills necessary to save our world: communication, cooperation, connecting and consensus building. If you choose to use these skills and to get involved in a cause, I salute you. But keep in mind that the greatest gift to the world is when you are just being your amazing and wonderful self. So, if that means painting a picture because that is what is in your heart, do it. If it means running for public office, do it. If it means having a baby, do it. Whatever is in your heart, whatever is authentically true for you, do that thing. And the world will smile.

Regardless of what you decide to do in your own life, please lend your vote and your voice to causes and changes that will help repair our tattered world.

Because if and when women come together to make change on a large scale, we could actually save the world.

And as for me, I'll be right there with you, doing my thing, being myself... and saving the world.